AMERICAN NOTES

Rudyard Kipling

AMERICAN NOTES

By
RUDYARD KIPLING

STANDARD BOOK COMPANY
LONDON   NEW YORK

"Punjab Edition"
ORSAMUS TURNER HARRIS
MCMXXX

American Notes

I

"Then spoke der Captain Stossenheim
Who had theories of God,
'Oh, Breitmann, this is judgment on
Der ways dot you have trod.
You only lifs to enjoy yourself
While you yourself agree
Dot self-development requires
Der religious Idee.' "

THIS is America.

They call her the *City of Peking,* and she belongs to the Pacific Mail Company, but for all practical purposes she is the United States.

We are divided between missionaries and generals—generals who were at Vicksburg and Shiloh, and German by birth, but more American than the Americans, who in confidence tell you that they are not generals at all, but only brevet majors of militia corps. The missionaries are perhaps the queerest portion of the cargo. Did you ever hear an English minister lecture for half an hour on the freight-traffic receipts and general working of, let us say, the Midland? The Professor has been sitting at the feet of a keen-eyed, close-bearded, swarthy man who expounded

unto him kindred mysteries with a fluency and
precision that a city leader-writer might have
envied. "Who's your financial friend with the
figures at his fingers' ends?" I asked. "Mission-
ary—Presbyterian Mission to the Japs," said the
professor. I laid my hand upon my mouth and
was dumb.

As a counterpoise to the missionaries, we carry
men from Manila—lean Scotchmen who gamble
once a month in the Manila State lottery and oc-
casionally turn up trumps. One, at least, drew
a ten-thousand-dollar prize last December and is
away to make merry in the New World. Everybody on the staff of an American steamer this
side the Continent seems to gamble steadily in
that lottery, and the talk of the smoking-room
runs almost entirely on prizes won by accident or
lost through a moment's delay. The tickets are
sold more or less openly at Yokohama and Hong-
Kong, and the drawings—losers and winners both
agree here—are above reproach.

We have resigned ourselves to the infinite
monotony of a twenty days' voyage. The Pacific
Mail advertises falsely. Only under the most
favorable circumstances of wind and steam can
their under-engined boats cover the distance in
fifteen days. Our *City of Peking,* for instance,
had been jogging along at a gentle ten knots an
hour, a pace out of all proportion to her bulk.
"When we get a wind," says the Captain, "we
shall do better." She is a four-master and can

carry any amount of canvas. It is not safe to run steamers across this void under the poles of Atlantic liners. The monotony of the sea is paralyzing. We have passed the wreck of a little sealing-schooner lying bottom up and covered with gulls. She weltered by in the chill dawn, unlovely as the corpse of a man; and the wild birds piped thinly at us as they steered her across the surges. The pulse of the Pacific is no little thing even in the quieter moods of the sea. It set our bows swinging and nosing and ducking ere we were a day clear of Yokohama, and yet there was never swell nor crested wave in sight. "We ride very high," said the Captain, "and she's a dry boat. She has a knack of crawling over things somehow; but we shan't need to put her to the test this journey."

* * * * * *

The Captain was mistaken. For four days we have endured the sullen displeasure of the North Pacific, winding up with a night of discomfort. It began with a gray sea, flying clouds, and a head-wind that smote fifty knots off the day's run. Then rose from the southeast a beam sea warranted by no wind that was abroad upon the waters in our neighborhood, and we wallowed in the trough of it for sixteen mortal hours. In the stillness of the harbor, when the newspaper man is lunching in her saloon and the steam-launch is crawling round her sides, a ship of pride is a "stately liner." Out in the open, one rugged shoulder of a sea between you and the horizon, she becomes "the old hooker," a "lively boat," and other things of small import, for this is necessary to propitiate the Ocean. "There's a storm to the southeast of us," explained the Captain. "That's what's kicking up this sea."

The *City of Peking* did not belie her reputation. She crawled over the seas in liveliest wise, never shipping a bucket till—she was forced to. Then she took it green over the bows to the vast edification of, at least, one passenger who had never seen the scuppers full before.

Later in the day the fun began. "Oh, she's a daisy at rolling," murmured the chief steward, flung starfish-wise on a table among his glassware. "She's rolling some," said a black apparition new risen from the stoke-hold. "Is she going to roll any more?" demanded the ladies grouped in what ought to have been the ladies' saloon, but, according to American custom, was labeled "Social Hall."

Passed in the twilight the chief officer—a dripping, bearded face. "Shall I mark out the bull-board?" said he, and lurched aft, followed by the tongue of a wave. "She'll roll her guards under to-night," said a man from Louisiana, where their river-steamers do not understand the meaning of bulwarks. We dined to a dashing accompaniment of crockery, the bounds of emancipated beer-bottles livelier than their own corks, and the clamor of the ship's gong broken loose and calling to meals on its own account.

After dinner the real rolling began. She did roll "guards under," as the Louisiana man had prophesied. At thirty-minute intervals to the second arrived one big sea, when the electric lamps died down to nothing, and the screw raved and the blows of the sea made the decks quiver. On those occasions we moved from our chairs, not gently, but discourteously. At other times we were merely holding on with both hands.

It was then that I studied Fear—Terror bound in black silk and fighting hard with herself. For reasons which will be thoroughly understood, there was a tendency among the passengers to herd together and to address inquiries to every officer who happened to stagger through the saloon. No one was in the least alarmed,—oh dear, no,—but all were keenly anxious for information. This anxiety redoubled after a more than usually vicious roll. Terror was a large, handsome, and cultured lady who knew the precise value of human life, the inwardness of *Robert Elsmere,* the latest poetry—everything in fact that a clever woman should know. When the rolling was near its worst, she began to talk swiftly. I do not for a moment believe that she knew what she was talking about. The rolling increased. She buckled down to the task of making conversation. By the heave of the laboring bust, the restless working of the fingers on the tablecloth, and the uncontrollable eyes that turned always to the companion stairhead, I was able to judge the extremity of her fear. Yet her words were frivolous and commonplace enough; they poured forth unceasingly, punctuated with little laughs and giggles, as a woman's speech should be. Presently, a member of her group suggested going to bed. No, she wanted to sit up; she wanted to go on talking, and as long as she could get a soul to sit with her she had her desire. When for sheer lack of company she was forced to get to her cabin, she left reluctantly, looking back to the well-lighted saloon over her shoulder. The contrast between the flowing triviality of her speech and the strained intentness of eye and hand was a quaint thing to behold. I know now how Fear should be painted.

No one slept very heavily that night. Both arms were needed to grip the berth, while the trunks below wound the carpet slips into knots and battered the framing of the cabins. Once it seemed to me that the whole of the laboring fabric that cased our trumpery fortunes stood on end and in this undignified posture hopped a mighty hop. Twice I know I shot out of my berth to join the adventurous trunks on the floor. A hundred times the crash of the wave on the ship's side was followed by the roar of the water, as it swept the decks and raved round the deckhouses. In a lull

grant Home Rule to the vermin in our blankets.
Then the real Americans will invite the Irish to
get up and git to where they came from. 'Wish
you'd hurry up that time before we have another
trouble. We're bound hand and foot by the Irish
vote; or at least that's the excuse for any unusual
theft that we perpetrate. I tell you there's no
good in an Irishman except as a fighter. He
doesn't understand work. He has a natural gift
of the gab, and he can drink a man blind. These
three qualifications make him a first-class politi-
cian."

With one accord the Americans present com-
menced to abuse Ireland and its people as they
had met them, and each man prefaced his
commination service with: "I am an American
by birth—an American from way back."

It must be an awful thing to live in a country
where you have to explain that you really belong
there. Louder grew the clamor and crisper the
sentiments.

"If we weren't among Americans, I should say
we were consorting with Russians," said a fellow-
countryman in my ear.

"They can't mean what they say," I whispered.
"Listen to this fellow."

"And I know, for I have been three times round
the world and resided in most countries on the
Continent, that there was never people yet could
govern themselves."

"Allah! This from an American!"

"And who should know better than an American?" was the retort. "For the ignorant—that is to say for the majority—there is only one argument—fear; the fear of Death. In our case we give any scallawag who comes across the water all the same privileges that we have made for ourselves. There we make a mistake. They thank us by playing the fool. Then we shoot them down. You can't persuade the mob of any country to become decent citizens. If they misbehave themselves, shoot them. I saw the bombs thrown at Chicago when our police were blown to bits. I saw the banners in the procession that threw the bombs. All the mottoes on them were in German. The men were aliens in our midst, and they were shot down like dogs. I've been in labor riots and seen the militia go through a crowd like a finger through tissue paper."

"I was in the riots at New Orleans," said the man from Louisiana. "We turned the Gatling on the other crowd, and they were sick."

"Whew! I wonder what would have happened if a Gatling had been used when the West End riots were in full swing?" said an Englishman. "If a single rioter were killed in an English town by the police, the chances are that the policeman would have to stand his trial for murder and the Ministry of the day would go out."

"Then you've got all your troubles before you. The more power you give the people, the more trouble they will give. With us our better classes are corrupt and our lower classes are lawless. There are millions of useful, law-abiding citizens, and they are very sick of this thing. We execute our justice in the streets. The law courts are no use. Take the case of the Chicago Anarchists. It was all we could do to get 'em hanged; whereas the dead in the streets had been punished offhand. We were sure of *them*. Guess that's the reason we are so quick to fire on a mob. But it's unfair, all the same. We receive all these cattle—Anarchists, Socialists, and ruffians of every sort—and then we shoot them. The States are as republican as they make 'em. We have no use for a man who wants to try any more experiments on the Constitution. We are the biggest people on God's earth. All the world knows that. We've been shouting that we are also the greatest people. No one cares to contradict us but ourselves; and we are now wondering whether we are what we claim to be. Never mind; you Britishers will have the same experiences to go through. You're beginning to rot now. Your County Councils will make you more rotten because you are putting power into the hands of untrained people. When you reach our level,—every man with a vote and the right to sell it; the right to nominate fellows of his own kidney to swamp out better men,—you'll be what we are now—rotten, rotten, rotten!"

The voice ceased, and no man rose up to contradict.

"We'll worry through it somehow," said the man from Louisiana. "What would do us a world of good now would be a big European war. We're getting slack and sprawly. Now a war outside our borders would make us all pull together. But that's a luxury we shan't get."

"Can't you raise one within your own borders?" I said flippantly, to get rid of the thought of the great blind nation in her unrest putting out her hand to the Sword. Mine was a most unfortunate remark.

"I hope not," said an American, very seriously. "We have paid a good deal to keep ourselves together before this, and it is not likely that we shall split up without protest. Yet some say that we are too large, and some say that Washington and the Eastern States are running the whole country. If ever we do divide,—God help us when we do,—it will be East and West this time."

"We built the old hooker too long in the run. Put the engine-room aft. Break her back," said an American who had not yet spoken. " 'Wonder if our forbears knew how she was going to grow."

"A very large country." The speaker sighed as though the weight of it from New York to 'Frisco lay upon his shoulders. "If ever we do divide, it means we are done for. There is no room for four first-class empires in the States. One split will lead to another if the first is successful.   What's the use of talking?"

What's the use?   Here's our conversation as it ran, the night of the Queen's Birthday.   What do *you* think?

II

"Serene, indifferent to fate,
Thou sittest at the western gate,
Thou seest the white seas fold their tents,
Oh warder of two Continents.
Thou drawest all things small and great
To thee beside the Western Gate."

THIS is what Bret Harte has written of the great city of San Francisco, and for the past fortnight I have been wondering what made him do it.

There is neither serenity nor indifference to be found in these parts; and evil would it be for the Continent whose wardship were intrusted to so reckless a guardian.

Behold me pitched neck-and-crop from twenty days of the High Seas, into the whirl of California, deprived of any guidance, and left to draw my own conclusions. Protect me from the wrath of an outraged community if these letters be ever read by American eyes. San Francisco is a mad city—inhabited for the most part by perfectly insane people whose women are of a remarkable beauty.

When the *City of Peking* steamed through the Golden Gate I saw with great joy that the block-house which guarded the mouth of the "finest harbor in the world, Sir," could be silenced by two gun-boats from Hong-Kong with safety, comfort, and despatch.

Then a reporter leaped aboard, and ere I could gasp held me in his toils. He pumped me exhaustively while I was getting ashore, demanding, of all things in the world, news about Indian journalism. It is an awful thing to enter a new land with a new lie on your lips. I spoke the truth to the evil-minded Custom-house man who turned my most sacred raiment on a floor composed of stable-refuse and pine-splinters; but the reporter overwhelmed me not so much by his poignant audacity as his beautiful ignorance. I am sorry now that I did not tell him more lies as I passed into a city of three hundred thousand white men. Think of it! Three hundred thousand white men and women gathered in one spot, walking upon real pavements in front of real plate-glass windowed shops, and talking something that was not very different from English. It was only when I had tangled myself up in a hopeless maze of small wooden houses, dust, street-refuse, and children who play with empty kerosene tins, that I discovered the difference of speech.

"You want to go to the Palace Hotel?" said an affable youth on a dray. "What in hell are you doing here, then? This is about the lowest place in the city. Go six blocks north to the corner of Geary and Market; then walk around till you strike corner of Gutter and Sixteenth, and that brings you there."

I do not vouch for the literal accuracy of these directions, quoting but from a disordered memory.

"Amen," I said. "But who am I that I should strike the corners of such as you name? Peradventure they be gentlemen of repute, and might hit back. Bring it down to dots, my son."

I thought he would have smitten me, but he didn't. He explained that no one ever used the word "street," and that every one was supposed to know how the streets run: for sometimes the names were upon the lamps and sometimes they weren't. Fortified with these directions I proceeded till I found a mighty street full of sumptuous buildings four or five stories high, but paved with rude cobble-stones in the fashion of the Year One. A cable-car without any visible means of support slid stealthily behind me and nearly struck me in the back. A hundred yards further there was a slight commotion in the street —a gathering together of three or four—and something glittered as it moved very swiftly. A ponderous Irish gentleman with priest's cords in his hat and a small nickel-plated badge on his fat bosom emerged from the knot, supporting a Chinaman who had been stabbed in the eye and was bleeding like a pig. The bystanders went their ways, and the Chinaman, assisted by the policeman, his own. Of course this was none of my business, but I rather wanted to know what had happened to the gentleman who had dealt the stab. It said a great deal for the excellence of the municipal arrangements of the town that a surging crowd did not at once block the street to see what was going forward. I was the sixth man and the last who assisted at the performance, and my curiosity was six times the greatest. Indeed, I felt ashamed of showing it.

There were no more incidents till I reached the Palace Hotel, a seven-storied warren of humanity with a thousand rooms in it. All the travel-books will tell you about hotel arrangements in this country. They should be seen to be appreciated. Understand clearly—and this letter is written after a thousand miles of experiences—that money will not buy you service in the West.

When the hotel clerk—the man who awards your room to you and who is supposed to give you information—when that resplendent individual stoops to attend to your wants, he does so whistling or humming, or picking his teeth, or pauses to converse with some one he knows. These performances, I gather, are to impress upon you that he is a free man and your equal. From his general appearance and the size of his diamonds he ought to be your superior. There is no necessity for this swaggering self-conscious-ness of freedom. Business is business, and the man who is paid to attend to a man might reasonably devote his whole attention to the job.

In a vast marble-paved hall under the glare of

an electric light sat forty or fifty men; and for their use and amusement were provided spittoons of infinite capacity and generous gape. Most of the men wore frock-coats and top-hats,—the things that we in India put on at a wedding breakfast if we possessed them,—but they all spat. They spat on principle. The spittoons were on the staircases, in each bedroom—yea, and in chambers even more sacred than these. They chased one into retirement, but they blossomed in chiefest splendor round the Bar, and they were all used, every reeking one of 'em.

Just before I began to feel deathly sick, another reporter grappled me. What he wanted to know was the precise area of India in square miles. I referred him to Whittaker. He had never heard of Whittaker. He wanted it from my own mouth, and I would not tell him. Then he swerved off, like the other man, to details of journalism in our own country. I ventured to suggest that the interior economy of a paper most concerned the people who worked it. "That's the very thing that interests us," he said. "Have you got reporters anything like our reporters on Indian newspapers?" "We have not," I said, and suppressed the "Thank God" rising to my lips. *"Why* haven't you?" said he. "Because they would die," I said. It was exactly like talking to a child—a very rude little child. He would begin almost every sentence with: "Now tell me something about India," and would turn aimlessly from one question to another without the least continuity. I was not angry, but keenly interested. The man was a revelation to me. To his questions I returned answers mendacious and evasive. After all, it really did not matter what I said. He could not understand. I can only hope and pray that none of the readers of the *Pioneer* will ever see that portentous interview. The man made me out to be an idiot several sizes more driveling than my destiny intended, and the rankness of his ignorance managed to distort the few poor facts with which I supplied him into large and elaborate lies. Then thought I: "The matter of American journalism shall be looked into later on. At present I will enjoy myself."

No man rose to tell me what were the lions of the place. No one volunteered any sort of conveyance. I was absolutely alone in this big city of white folk. By instinct I sought refreshment and came upon a bar-room, full of bad Salon pictures, in which men with hats on the backs of their heads were wolfing food from a counter. It was the institution of the "Free Lunch" that I had struck. You paid for a drink and got as much as you wanted to eat. For something less than a rupee a day a man can feed himself sumptuously in San Francisco, even though he be bankrupt. Remember this if ever you are stranded in these parts.

Later, I began a vast but unsystematic exploration of the streets. I asked for no names. It

was enough that the pavements were full of white
men and women, the streets clanging with traffic,
and that the restful roar of a great city rang in
my ears. The cable-cars glided to all points of
the compass. I took them one by one till I could
go no farther. San Francisco has been pitched
down on the sand bunkers of the Bikaneer desert.
About one-fourth of it is ground reclaimed from
the sea—any old-timer will tell you all about that.
The remainder is ragged, unthrifty sand-hills,
pegged down by houses.

From an English point of view there has not
been the least attempt at grading those hills,
and indeed you might as well try to grade the
hillocks of Sind. The cable-cars have for all practical purposes made San Francisco a dead level.
They take no count of rise or fall, but slide equably
on their appointed courses from one end to the
other of a six-mile street. They turn corners almost
at right angles; cross other lines, and, for aught
I know, may run up the sides of houses. There is
no visible agency of their flight; but once in a
while you shall pass a five-storied building, humming with machinery that winds up an everlasting
wire-cable, and the initiated will tell you that here
is the mechanism. I gave up asking questions. If
it pleases Providence to make a car run up and
down a slit in the ground for many miles, and if
for twopence-halfpenny I can ride in that car, why
shall I seek the reasons of the miracle? Rather
let me look out of the windows till the shops

give place to thousands and thousands of little houses made of wood—each house just big enough for a man and his family. Let me watch the people in the cars, and try to find out in what manner they differ from us, their ancestors.

They delude themselves into the belief that they talk English,—*the* English,—and I have already been pitied for speaking with "an English Accent." The man who pitied me spoke, so far as I was concerned, the language of thieves. And they all do. Where we put the accent forward, they throw it back, and *vice versa;* where we use the long *a,* they use the short; and words so simple as to be past mistaking, they pronounce somewhere up in the dome of their heads. How do these things happen?

Oliver Wendell Holmes says that Yankee schoolmarms, the cider, and the salt codfish of the Eastern States are responsible for what he calls a nasal accent. A Hindu is a Hindu, and a brother to the man who knows his vernacular; and a Frenchman is French because he speaks his own language; but the American has no language. He is dialect, slang, provincialism, accent, and so forth. Now that I have heard their voices, all the beauty of Bret Harte is being ruined for me, because I find myself catching through the roll of his rhythmical prose the cadence of his peculiar fatherland. Get an American lady to read to you "How Santa Clause came to Simpson's Bar," and

see how much is, under her tongue, left of the
beauty of the original.

But I am sorry for Bret Harte. It happened
this way. A reporter asked me what I thought
of the city, and I made answer suavely that
it was hallowed ground to me because of Bret
Harte. That was true.

"Well," said the reporter, "Bret Harte claims
California, but California don't claim Bret Harte.
He's been so long in England that he's quite English. Have you seen our cracker-factories and
the new offices of the *Examiner?*" He could not
understand that to the outside world the city was
worth a great deal less than the man.

*   *   *   *   *   *

Night fell over the Pacific, and the white sea-
fog whipped through the streets, dimming the
splendors of the electric lights. It is the use of
this city, her men and women, to parade between
the hours of eight and ten a certain street, called
Kearney Street, where the finest shops are sit-
uated. Here the click of heels on the pavement
is loudest, here the lights are brightest, and here
the thunder of the traffic is most overwhelming.
I watched Young California and saw that it was
at least expensively dressed, cheerful in manner,
and self-asserting in conversation. Also the
women are very fair. The maidens were of generous build, large, well-groomed, and attired in
raiment that even to my inexperienced eyes must

have cost much. Kearney Street, at nine o'clock, levels all distinctions of rank as impartially as the grave. Again and again I loitered at the heels of a couple of resplendent beings, only to overhear, when I expected the level voice of culture, the *staccato* "Sez he," "Sez I," that is the mark of the white servant-girl all the world over.

This was depressing because, in spite of all that goes to the contrary, fine feathers ought to make fine birds. There was wealth—unlimited wealth—in the streets, but not an accent that would have been dear at fifty cents. Wherefore, revolving in my mind that these folk were barbarians, I was presently enlightened and made aware that they also were the heirs of all the ages, and civilized after all. There appeared before me an affable stranger of prepossessing appearance, with a blue and an innocent eye. Addressing me by name, he claimed to have met me in New York at the Windsor, and to this claim I gave a qualified assent. I did not remember the fact, but since he was so certain of it, why then —I waited developments.

"And what did you think of Indiana when you came through?" was the next question.

It revealed the mystery of previous acquaintance, and one or two other things. With reprehensible carelessness, my friend of the light-blue eye had looked up the name of his victim in the hotel register and read "India" for Indiana.

He could not imagine an Englishman coming

through the States from West to East instead of by the regularly ordained route. My fear was that in his delight at finding me so responsive he would make remarks about New York and the Windsor which I could not understand. And indeed, he adventured in this direction once or twice, asking me what I thought of such and such streets, which, from his tone, I gathered were anything but respectable. It is trying to talk unknown New York in almost unknown San Francisco. But my friend was merciful. He protested that I was one after his own heart, and pressed upon me rare and curious drinks at more than one bar. These drinks I accepted with gratitude, as also the cigars with which his pockets were stored. He would show me the Life of the city. Having no desire to watch a weary old play again, I evaded the offer, and received in lieu of the Devil's instruction much coarse flattery. Curiously constituted is the soul of man. Knowing how and where this man lied; waiting idly for the finale; I was distinctly conscious, as he bubbled compliments in my ear, of soft thrills of gratified pride. I was wise quoth he, anybody could see that with half an eye; sagacious; versed in the affairs of the world; an acquaintance to be desired; one who had tasted the cup of Life with discretion.

All this pleased me, and in a measure numbed the suspicion that was thoroughly aroused. Eventually the blue-eyed one discovered, nay insisted, that I had a taste for cards (this was clumsily worked in, but it was my fault, in that I met him half-way, and allowed him no chance of good acting). Hereupon, I laid my head to one side, and simulated unholy wisdom, quoting odds and ends of poker-talk, all ridiculously misapplied. My friend kept his countenance admirably; and well he might, for five minutes later we arrived, always by the purest of chances, at a place where we could play cards, and also frivol with Louisiana State Lottery tickets. Would I play?

"Nay," said I, "for to me cards have neither meaning nor continuity; but let us assume that I am going to play. How would you and your friends get to work? Would you play a straight game or make me drunk, or—well, the fact is I'm a newspaper man, and I'd be much obliged if you'd let me know something about bunco-steering."

My blue-eyed friend cursed me by his gods, —the Right and the Left Bower; he even cursed the very good cigars he had given me. But, the storm over, he quieted down and explained. I apologized for causing him to waste an evening, and we spent a very pleasant time together.

Inaccuracy, provincialism, and a too hasty rushing to conclusions were the rocks that he had split on; but he got his revenge when he said:

"How would I play with you? From all the poppycock" (*Anglice,* bosh) "you talked about poker, I'd ha' played a straight game and skinned you. I wouldn't have taken the trouble to make you drunk. You never knew anything of the game; but the way I was mistaken in you makes me sick."

He glared at me as though I had done him an injury. To-day I know how it is that, year after year, week after week, the bunco-steerer, who is the confidence-trick and the card-sharper of other climes, secures his prey. He slavers them with flattery, as the snake slavers the rabbit. The incident depressed me because it showed I had left the innocent East far behind, and was come to a country where a man must look out for himself. The very hotel glistened with notices about keeping my door locked, and depositing my valuables in a safe. The white man in a lump is bad. Weeping softly for O-Toyo (little I knew then that my heart was to be torn afresh from my bosom!), I fell asleep in the clanging hotel.

Next morning I had entered upon the Deferred Inheritance. There are no princes in America,— at least with crowns on their heads,—but a generous-minded member of some royal family received my letter of introduction. Ere the day closed I was a member of the two clubs and booked for many engagements to dinner and party. Now this prince, upon whose financial operations be continual increase, had no reason, nor had the others, his friends, to put himself out for the sake of one Briton more or less; but he rested not till he had accomplished all in my behalf that a mother could think of for her *débu-tante* daughter. Do you know the Bohemian Club of San Francisco? They say its fame extends over the world. It was created somewhat on the lines of the Savage by men who wrote or drew things, and it has blossomed into most un-republican luxury. The ruler of the place is an owl—an owl standing upon a skull and cross-bones, showing forth grimly the wisdom of the man of letters and the end of his hopes for im-mortality. The owl stands on the staircase, a statue four feet high, is carved in the woodwork, flutters on the frescoed ceilings, is stamped on the note-paper, and hangs on the walls. He is an Ancient and Honorable Bird. Under his wing 'twas my privilege to meet with white men whose lives were not chained down to routine of toil, who wrote magazine articles instead of reading them hurriedly in the pauses of office-work, who painted pictures instead of contenting themselves with cheap etchings picked up at another man's sale of effects. Mine were all the rights of social intercourse that India, stony-hearted stepmother of Collectors, has swindled us out of. Treading soft carpets and breathing the incense of superior cigars, I wandered from room to room studying the paintings in which the members of the Club had caricatured themselves, their associates, and their aims. There was a slick French audacity about the workmanship of these men of toil un-bending that went straight to the heart of the beholder. And yet it was not altogether French. A dry grimness of treatment, almost Dutch, marked the difference. The men painted as they spoke—with certainty. The club indulges in revelries which it calls "jinks"—high and low, —at intervals,—and each of these gatherings is faithfully portrayed in oils by hands that know their business. In this club were no amateurs spoiling canvas because they fancied they could handle oils without knowledge of shadows or anatomy—no gentleman of leisure ruining the temper of publishers and an already ruined market with attempts to write "because everybody writes something these days."

My hosts were working, or had worked, for their daily bread with pen or paint, and their talk for the most part was of the shop shoppy—that is to say, delightful. They extended a large hand of welcome and were as brethren, and I did homage to the Owl and listened to their talk. An Indian Club about Christmas-time will yield, if properly worked, an abundant harvest of queer tales; but at a gathering of Americans from the uttermost ends of their own continent the tales are larger, thicker, more spinous, and even more azure than any Indian variety. Tales of the War I heard told by an ex-officer of the South over his evening drink to a Colonel of the Northern army; my introducer, who had served as a trooper in the Northern Horse, throwing in emendations from time to time.

Other voices followed with equally wondrous tales of riata-throwing in Mexico or Arizona, of gambling at army posts in Texas, of newspaper wars waged in godless Chicago, of deaths sudden and violent in Montana and Dakota, of the loves of half-breed maidens in the South, and fantastic huntings for gold in mysterious Alaska. Above all, they told the story of the building of old San Francisco, when the "finest collection of humanity on God's earth, Sir, started this town, and the water came up to the foot of Market Street." Very terrible were some of the tales, grimly humorous the others, and the men in broadcloth and fine linen who told them had played their parts in them.

"And now and again when things got too bad they would toll the city bell, and the Vigilance Committee turned out and hanged the suspicious characters. A man didn't begin to be suspected in those days till he had committed at least one unprovoked murder," said a calm-eyed, portly old gentleman.

I looked at the pictures around me, the noiseless, neat-uniformed waiter behind me, the oakribbed ceiling above, the velvety carpet beneath. It was hard to realize that even twenty years ago you could see a man hanged with great pomp. Later on I found reason to change my opinion. The tales gave me a headache and set me thinking. How in the world was it possible to take in even one-thousandth of this huge, roaring, many-sided continent? In the silence of the sumptuous library lay Professor Bryce's book on the American Republic.

"It is an omen," said I. "He has done all things in all seriousness, and he may be purchased for half a guinea. Those who desire information of the most undoubted must refer to his pages. For me is the daily round of vagabondage, the recording of the incidents of the hour, and talk with the traveling companion of the day. I will not 'do' this country at all."

And I forgot all about India for ten days while I went out to dinners and watched the social customs of the people, which are entirely different from our customs, and was introduced to the men of many millions. These persons are harmless in their earlier stages; that is to say, a man worth three or four million dollars may be a good talker, clever, amusing, and of the world; a man with twice that amount is to be avoided; and a twenty-million man is—just twenty millions. Take an instance. I was speaking to a newspaper man about seeing the proprietor of his journal. My friend snorted indignantly:

"See *him!* Great Scott! *No!* If he happens to appear in the office, I have to associate with him; but, thank Heaven, outside of that I move in circles where he cannot come."

And yet the first thing I have been taught to believe is that money was everything in America!

III

"Poor men—God made, and all for that!"

IT was a bad business throughout, and the only consolation is that it was all my fault.

A man took me round the Chinese quarter of San Francisco, which is a ward of the city of Canton set down in the most eligible business-quarter of the place.

The Chinaman with his usual skill has possessed himself of good brick fire-proof buildings and, following instinct, has packed each tenement with hundreds of souls, all living in filth and squalor not to be appreciated save by you in India. That cursory investigation ought to have sufficed; but I wanted to know how deep in the earth the Pig-tail had taken root. Therefore I explore the Chinese quarter a second time and alone, which was foolishness. No one in the filthy streets (but for the blessed sea breezes San Francisco would enjoy cholera every season) interfered with my movements, though many asked for *cumshaw*. I struck a house about four stories high full of celestial abominations, and began to burrow down; having heard that these tenements were constructed on the lines of icebergs—two-thirds below sight level. Downstairs I crawled past Chinamen in bunks, opium-smokers, brothels, and gambling hells, till I had reached the second cellar—was, in fact, in the labyrinths of a warren. Great is the wisdom of the Chinaman. In time of trouble that house could be razed to the ground by the mob, and yet hide all its inhabitants in brick-walled and wooden-beamed subterranean galleries, strengthened with iron-framed doors and gates. On the second underground floor a man asked for *cumshaw* and took me down-stairs to yet another cellar, where the air was as thick as butter, and the lamps burned little holes in it not more than an inch square. In this place a poker club had assembled and was in full swing. The Chinaman loves "pokel," and plays it with great skill, swearing like a cat when he loses. Most of the men round the table were in semi-European dress, their pig-tails curled up under billy-cock hats. One of the company looked like a Eurasian, whence I argued that he was a Mexican—a supposition that later inquiries confirmed. They were a picturesque set of fiends and polite, being too absorbed in their game to look at the stranger. We were all deep down under the earth, and save for the rustle of a blue gown sleeve and the ghostly whisper of the cards as they were shuffled and played, there was no sound. The heat was almost unendurable. There was some dispute between the Mexican and the man on his left. The latter shifted his place to put the table between himself and his opponent, and stretched a lean yellow hand towards the Mexican's winnings.

Mark how purely man is a creature of instinct. Rarely introduced to the pistol, I saw the Mexican half rise in his chair and at the same instant found myself full length on the floor. None had told me that this was the best attitude when bullets are abroad. I was there prone before I had time to think—dropping as the room was filled with an intolerable clamor like the discharge of a canon. In those close quarters the pistol report had no room to spread any more than the smoke—then acrid in my nostrils. There was no second shot, but a great silence in which I rose slowly to my knees. The Chinaman was gripping the table with both hands and staring in front of him at an empty chair. The Mexican had gone, and a little whirl of smoke was floating near the roof. Still gripping the table, the Chinaman said: "Ah!" in the tone that a man would use when, looking up from his work suddenly, he sees a well-known friend in the doorway. Then he coughed and fell over to his own right, and I saw that he had been shot in the stomach.

I became aware that, save for two men leaning over the stricken one, the room was empty; and all the tides of intense fear, hitherto held back by intenser curiosity, swept over my soul. I ardently desired the outside air. It was possible that the Chinamen would mistake me for the

Mexican,—everything horrible seemed possible just then,—and it was more than possible that the stairways would be closed while they were hunting for the murderer. The man on the floor coughed a sickening cough. I heard it as I fled, and one of his companions turned out the lamp. Those stairs seemed interminable, and to add to my dismay there was no sound of commotion in the house. No one hindered, no one even looked at me. There was no trace of the Mexican. I found the doorway and, my legs trembling under me, reached the protection of the clear cool night, the fog, and the rain. I dared not run, and for the life of me I could not walk. I must have effected a compromise, for I remember the light of a street lamp showed the shadow of one half skipping—caracoling along the pavements in what seemed to be an ecstasy of suppressed happiness. But it was fear—deadly fear. Fear compounded of past knowledge of the Oriental—only other white man—available witness—three stories underground—and the cough of the Chinaman now some forty feet under my clattering boot-heels. It was good to see the shop-fronts and electric lights again. Not for anything would I have informed the police, because I firmly believed that the Mexican had been dealt with somewhere down there on the third floor long ere I had reached the air; and, moreover, once clear of the place, I could not for the life of me tell where it was. My ill-considered flight brought me out

somewhere a mile distant from the hotel; and
the clank of the lift that bore me to a bed six
stories above ground was music in my ears.
Wherefore I would impress it upon you who follow after, do not knock about the Chinese
quarters at night and alone. You may stumble
across a picturesque piece of human nature that
will unsteady your nerves for half a day.

*   *   *   *   *   *

And this brings me by natural sequence to
the great drink question. As you know, of course,
the American does not drink at meals as a sensible
man should. Indeed, he has no meals. He stuffs
for ten minutes thrice a day. Also he has no
decent notions about the sun being over the yard-
arm or below the horizon. He pours his vanity
into himself at unholy hours, and indeed he can
hardly help it. You have no notion of what "treating" means on the Western slope. It is more than
an institution; it is a religion, though men tell me
that it is nothing to what it was. Take a very
common instance. At 10.30 A. M. a man is smitten with a desire for stimulants. He is in the
company of two friends. All three adjourn to
the nearest bar,—seldom more than twenty yards
away,—and take three straight whiskies. They
talk for two minutes. The second and third man
then treats in order; and thus each walks into the
street, two of them the poorer by three goes of

whisky under their belt and one with two more
liquors than he wanted. It is not etiquette yet
to refuse a treat. The result is peculiar. I have
never yet, I confess, seen a drunken man in the
streets, but I have heard more about drunkenness
among white men, and seen more decent men
above or below themselves with drink, than I care
to think about. And the vice runs up into all
sorts of circles and societies. Never was I more
astonished than at one pleasant dinner party to
hear a pair of pretty lips say casually of a gentleman friend then under discussion, "He was
drunk." The fact was merely stated without
emotion. That was what startled me. But the
climate of California deals kindly with excess,
and treacherously covers up its traces. A man
neither bloats nor shrivels in this dry air. He
continues with the false bloom of health upon his
cheeks, an equable eye, a firm mouth, and a steady
hand till a day of reckoning arrives, and suddenly
breaking up, about the head, he dies, and his
friends speak his epitaph accordingly. Why people who in most cases cannot hold their liquor
should play with it so recklessly I leave to others
to decide. This unhappy state of affairs has,
however, produced one good result which I will
confide to you. In the heart of the business
quarter, where banks and bankers are thickest,
and telegraph wires most numerous, stands a
semi-subterranean bar tended by a German with
long blond locks and a crystalline eye. Go thither

softly, treading on the tips of your toes, and ask him for a Button Punch. 'Twill take ten minutes to brew, but the result is the highest and noblest product of the age. No man but one knows what is in it. I have a theory it is compounded of the shavings of cherubs' wings, the glory of a tropical dawn, the red clouds of sunset, and fragments of lost epics by dead masters. But try you for yourselves, and pause a while to bless me, who am always mindful of the truest interests of my brethren.

But enough of the stale spilth of bar-rooms. Turn now to the august spectacle of a Government of the people, by the people, for the people, as it is understood in the city of San Francisco. Professor Bryce's book will tell you that every American citizen over twenty-one years of age possesses a vote. He may not know how to run his own business, control his wife, or instill reverence into his children, may be pauper, half-crazed with drink, bankrupt, dissolute, or merely a born fool; but he has a vote. If he likes, he can be voting most of his time—voting for his State Governor, his municipal officers, local option, sewage contracts, or anything else of which he has no special knowledge.

Once every four years he votes for a new President. In his spare moments he votes for his own judges—the men who shall give him justice. These are dependent on popular favor for re-election inasmuch as they are but chosen for a term of years—two or three, I believe. Such a position is manifestly best calculated to create an independent and unprejudiced administrator. Now this mass of persons who vote is divided into two parties—Republican and Democrat. They are both agreed in thinking that the other part is running creation (which is America) into red flame. Also the Democrat as a party drinks more than the Republican, and when drunk may be heard to talk about a thing called the Tariff, which he does not understand, but which he conceives to be the bulwark of the country or else the surest power for its destruction. Sometimes he says one thing and sometimes another, in order to contradict the Republican, who is always contradicting himself. And this is a true and lucid account of the forepart of American politics. The behind-part is otherwise.

Since every man has a vote and may vote on every conceivable thing, it follows that there exist certain wise men who understand the art of buying up votes retail, and vending them wholesale to whoever wants them most urgently. Now an American engaged in making a home for himself has not time to vote for turncocks and district attorneys and cattle of that kind, but the unemployed have much time because they are always on hand somewhere in the streets. They are called "the boys," and form a peculiar class. The boys are young men; inexpert in war, unskilled in labor; who have neither killed a man, lifted cattle, or dug a well. In plain English, they are just the men in the streets who can always be trusted to rally round any cause that has a glass of liquor for a visible heart. They wait—they are on hand—; and in being on hand lies the crown and the glory of American politics. The wise man is he who, keeping a liquor saloon and judiciously dispensing drinks, knows how to retain within arm's reach a block of men who will vote for or against anything under the canopy of Heaven. Not every saloon-keeper can do this. It demands careful study of city politics, tact, the power of conciliation, and infinite resources of anecdote to amuse and keep the crowd together night after night, till the saloon becomes a salon. Above all, the liquor side of the scheme must not be worked for immediate profit. The boys who drink so freely will ultimately pay their host a thousandfold. An Irishman, and an Irishman pre-eminently, knows how to work such a saloon parliament. Observe for a moment the plan of operations. The rank and file are treated to drink and a little money—and they vote. He who controls ten votes receives a proportionate reward; the dispenser of a thousand votes is worthy of reverence, and so the chain runs on till we reach the most successful worker of public saloons—the man most skillful in keeping his items together and using them when required. Such a man governs the city as absolutely as a king. And you would know where the gain comes in? The whole of the public offices of a city (with the exception of a very few where special technical skill is required) are short-term offices distributed according to "political" leanings. What would you have? A big city requires many officials. Each office carries a salary and influence worth twice the pay. The offices are for the representatives of the men who keep together and are on hand to vote. The Commissioner of Sewage, let us say, is a gentleman who has been elected to his office by a Republican vote. He knows little and cares less about sewage, but he has sense enough to man the pumping-works and the street-sweeping machines with the gentlemen who elected him. The Commissioner of Police has been helped to his post very largely by the influence of the boys at such and such a saloon. He may be the guardian of city morals, but he is not going to allow his subordinates to enforce early closing or abstention from gambling in that saloon. Most offices are limited to four years, consequently he is a fool who does not make his office pay him while he is in it.

The only people who suffer by this happy arrangement are, in fact, the people who devise the lovely system. And they suffer because they are Americans. Let us explain. As you know, every big city here holds at least one big foreign vote—generally Irish, frequently German. In San Francisco, the gathering place of the races, there is a distinct Italian vote to be considered,

but the Irish vote is more important. For this
reason the Irishman does not kill himself with
overwork. He is made for the cheery dispensing
of liquors, for everlasting blarney, and possesses
a wonderfully keen appreciation of the weaknesses
of lesser human nature. Also he has no sort of
conscience, and only one strong conviction—that
of deep-rooted hatred toward England. He keeps
to the streets, he is on hand, he votes joyously,
spending days lavishly,—and time is the American's dearest commodity. Behold the glorious result. To-day the city of San Francisco is gov-
erned by the Irish vote and the Irish influence,
under the rule of a gentleman whose sight is im-
paired, and who requires a man to lead him about
the streets. He is called officially "Boss Buckley," and unofficially the "Blind White Devil."
I have before me now the record of his amiable
career in black and white. It occupies four col-
umns of small print, and perhaps you would think
it disgraceful. Summarized, it is as follows:
Boss Buckley, by tact and deep knowledge of the
seamy side of the city, won himself a following
of voters. He sought no office himself, or rarely:
but as his following increased he sold their services to the highest bidder, himself taking toll of
the revenues of every office. He controlled the
Democratic party in the city of San Francisco.
The people appoint their own judges. Boss
Buckley's people appointed judges. These judges
naturally were Boss Buckley's property. I have

been to dinner parties and heard educated men, not concerned with politics, telling stories one to another of "justice," both civil and criminal, being bought with a price from the hands of these judges. Such tales they told without heat, as men recording facts. Contracts for roadmending, public buildings, and the like are under the control of Boss Buckley, because the men whom Buckley's following sent to the City Council adjudicate on these contracts; and on each and every one of these contracts Boss Buckley levies his percentage for himself and his allies.

The Republican party in San Francisco also have their boss. He is not so great a genius as Boss Buckley, but I decline to believe that he is any whit more virtuous. He has a smaller number of votes at his command.

IV

I HAVE been watching machinery in repose after reading about machinery in action.

An excellent gentleman who bears a name honored in the magazines writes, much as Disraeli orated, of "the sublime instincts of an ancient people," the certainty with which they can be trusted to manage their own affairs in their own way, and the speed with which they are making for all sorts of desirable goals. This he called a statement or purview of American politics.

I went almost directly afterwards to a saloon where gentlemen interested in ward politics nightly congregate. They were not pretty persons. Some if them were bloated, and they all swore cheerfully till the heavy gold watch-chains on their fat stomachs rose and fell again; but they talked over their liquor as men who had power and unquestioned access to places of trust and profit.

The magazine-writer discussed theories of government; these men the practice. They had been there. They knew all about it. They banged their fist on the table and spoke of political "pulls," the vending of votes, and so forth. Theirs was not the talk of village babblers reconstructing the affairs of the nation, but of strong, coarse, lust-

ful men fighting for spoil and thoroughly under-
standing the best methods of reaching it. I listened long and intently to speech I could not
understand, or only in spots. It was the speech
of business, however. I had sense enough to
know *that,* and to do my laughing outside the
door. Then I began to understand why my pleasant and well-educated hosts in San Francisco
spoke with bitter scorn of such duties of citizen-
ship as voting and taking an interest in the
distribution of offices. Scores of men have told
me with no false pride that they would as soon
concern themselves with the public affairs of the
City or State as rake muck. Read about politics
as the cultured writer of the magazines regards
'em, and then, *and not till then,* pay your respects
to the gentlemen who run the grimy reality.

I'm sick of interviewing night-editors, who, in
response to my demand for the record of a
prominent citizen, answers: "Well, you see, he
began by keeping a saloon," etc. I prefer to believe that my informants are treating me as in
the old sinful days in India I was used to treat
our wandering Globe-trotters. They declare that
they speak the truth, and the news of dog-politics
lately vouchsafed to me in groggeries incline me
to believe—but I won't. The people are much too
nice to slangander as recklessly as I have been
doing. Besides, I am hopelessly in love with
about eight American maidens—all perfectly delightful till the next one comes into the room.

O-Toyo was a darling, but she lacked several things; conversation, for one. You cannot live on giggles. She shall remain unmoved at Nagasaki while I roast a battered heart before the shrine of a big Kentucky blonde who had for a nurse, when she was little, a negro "mammy." By consequence she has welded on to California beauty, Paris dresses, Eastern culture, Europe trips, and wild Western originality, the queer dreamy superstitions of the negro quarters, and the result is soul-shattering. And she is but one of many stars. *Item*, a maiden who believes in education and possesses it, with a few hundred thousand dollars to boot, and a taste for slumming. *Item*, the leader of a sort of informal salon where girls congregate, read papers, and daringly discuss metaphysical problems and candy —a sloe-eyed, black-browed imperious maiden. *Item*, a very small maiden, absolutely without reverence, who can in one swift sentence trample upon and leave gasping half a dozen young men. *Item*, a millionairess, burdened with her money, lonely, caustic, with a tongue keen as a sword, yearning for a sphere, but chained up to the rock of her vast possessions. *Item*, a typewriter-maiden earning her own bread in this big city, because she doesn't think a girl ought to be a burden on her parents. She quotes Théophile Gautier, and moves through the world manfully, much respected, for all her twenty inexperienced summers. *Item*, a woman from Cloudland who has

no history in the past, but is discreetly of the
present, and strives for the confidences of male
humanity on the grounds of "sympathy." (This
is not altogether a new type.) *Item,* a girl in
a "dive" blessed with a Greek head and eyes that
seem to speak all that is best and sweetest in the
world. But woe is me!—she has no ideas in this
world or the next, beyond the consumption of
beer (a commission on each bottle), and protests
that she sings the songs allotted to her nightly
with no more than the vaguest notion of their
meaning.

Sweet and comely are the maidens of Devon-
shire; delicate and of gracious seeming those
who live in the pleasant places of London; fascinating for all their demureness the damsels of
France clinging closely to their mothers, and with
large eyes wondering at the wicked world; excellent in her own place and to those who understand her is the Anglo-Indian "spin" in her second
season; but the girls of America are above and
beyond them all. They are clever; they can talk.
Yea, it is said that they think. Certainly they
have an appearance of so doing. They are
original, and look you between the brows with un-
abashed eyes as a sister might look at her brother.
They are instructed in the folly and vanity of the
male mind, for they have associated with "the
boys" from babyhood, and can discerningly minister to both vices, or pleasantly snub the possessor. They possess, moreover, a life among

themselves, independent of masculine associations.
They have societies and clubs and unlimited tea-
fights where all the guests are girls. They are
self-possessed without parting with any tender-
ness that is their sex-right; they understand; they
can take care of themselves; they are superbly
independent. When you ask them what makes
them so charming, they say: "It is because we
are better educated than your girls and—and
we are more sensible in regard to men. We have
good times all around, but we aren't taught to
regard every man as a possible husband. Nor is
he expected to marry the first girl he calls on
regularly." Yes, they have good times, their free-
dom is large, and they do not abuse it. They can
go driving with young men, and receive visits
from young men to an extent that would make an
English mother wink with horror; and neither
driver nor drivee have a thought beyond the enjoyment of a good time. As certain also of their
own poets have said:—

> "Man is fire and woman is tow,
> And the devil he comes and begins to blow."

In America the tow is soaked in a solution that
makes it fireproof, in absolute liberty and large
knowledge: consequently accidents do not exceed
the regular percentage arranged by the Devil
for each class and climate under the skies. But
the freedom of the young girl has its drawbacks.

She is—I say it with all reluctance—irreverent, from her forty-dollar bonnet to the buckles in her eighteen-dollar shoes. She talks flippantly to her parents and men old enough to be her grandfather. She has a prescriptive right to the society of the Man who Arrives. The parents admit it. This is sometimes embarrassing, especially when you call on a man and his wife for the sake of information; the one being a merchant of varied knowledge, the other a woman of the world. In five minutes your host has vanished. In another five his wife has followed him, and you are left with a very charming maiden doubtless, but certainly not the person you came to see. She chatters and you grin; but you leave with the very strong impression of a wasted morning. This has been my experience once or twice. I have even said as pointedly as I dared to a man: "I came to see you." "You'd better see me in my office, then. The house belongs to my womenfolk—to my daughter, that is to say." He spoke with truth. The American of wealth is owned by his family. They exploit him for bullion, and sometimes it seems to me that his lot is a lonely one. The women get the ha'pence; the kicks are all his own. Nothing is too good for an American's daughter (I speak here of the moneyed classes). The girls take every gift as a matter of course. Yet they develop greatly when a catastrophe arrives and the man of many millions goes up or goes down and his daughters take to

is a fairy tale. You can read it in books. You would never believe me. All manner of nourishing food from sea-fish to beef may be bought at the lowest prices; and the people are well developed and of a high stomach. They demand ten shillings for tinkering a jammed lock of a trunk; they receive sixteen shillings a day for working as carpenters; they spend many sixpences on very bad cigars, and they go mad over a prize-fight. When they disagree, they do so fatally, with fire-arms in their hands, and on the public streets. I was just clear of Mission Street when the trouble began between two gentlemen, one of whom perforated the other. When a policeman, whose name I do not recollect, "fatally shot Ed. Kearney," for attempting to escape arrest, I was in the next street. For these things I am thankful. It is enough to travel with a policeman in a tram-car and while he arranges his coat-tails as he sits down, to catch sight of a loaded revolver. It is enough to know that fifty per cent. of the men in the public saloons carry pistols about them. The Chinaman waylays his adversary and methodically chops him to pieces with his hatchet. Then the Press roar about the brutal ferocity of the Pagan. The Italian reconstructs his friend with a long knife. The Press complains of the waywardness of the alien. The Irishman and the native Californian in their hours of discontent use the revolver, not once, but six times. The Press records the fact, and asks in the next column whether the world can parallel the progress of San Francisco. The American who loves his country will tell you that this sort of thing is confined to the lower classes. Just at present an ex-judge who was sent to jail by another judge (upon my word, I cannot tell whether these titles mean anything) is breathing red-hot vengeance against his enemy. The papers have interviewed both parties and confidently expect a fatal issue.

Now let me draw breath and curse the negro waiter and through him the negro in service generally. He has been made a citizen with a vote; consequently both political parties play with him. But that is neither here nor there. He will commit in one meal every *bétise* that a scullion fresh from the plowtail is capable of, and he will continue to repeat those faults. He is as complete a heavy-footed, uncomprehending, bungle-fisted fool as any *memsahib* in the East ever took into her establishment. But he is according to law a free and independent citizen—consequently above reproof or criticism. He, and he alone, in this insane city will wait at table (the Chinaman doesn't count). He is untrained, inept, but he will fill the place and draw the pay. Now God and his father's Kismet made him intellectually inferior to the Oriental. He insists on pretending that he serves tables by accident—as a sort of amusement. He wishes you to understand this little fact. You wish to eat your meals, and if possible to have them properly served. He is a

big, black, vain baby and a man rolled into one.
A colored gentleman who insisted on getting me
pie when I wanted something else, demanded information about India. I gave him some facts
about wages. "Oh hell," said he, cheerfully, "that
wouldn't keep me in cigars for a month." Then
he fawned on me for a ten-cent piece. Later he
took it upon himself to pity the natives of India
—"heathen" he called them, this Woolly One
whose race has been the butt of every comedy on
the Asiatic stage since the beginning. And I
turned and saw by the head upon his shoulders
that he was a Yoruba man, if there be any truth
in ethnological castes. He did his thinking in
English, but he was a Yoruba negro, and the race
type had remained the same throughout his gen-
erations. And the room was full of other races—
some that looked exactly like Gallas (but the
trade was never recruited from that side of
Africa), some duplicates of Cameroon heads, and
some Kroomen, if ever Kroomen wore evening
dress. The American does not consider little
matters of descent, though by this time he ought
to know all about "damnable heredity." As a
general rule he keeps himself very far from the
negro and says unpretty things about him. There
are six million negroes more or less in the States,
and they are increasing. The Americans once
having made them citizens cannot unmake them.
He says, in his newspapers, they ought to be ele-
vated by education. He is trying this: but it is

like to be a long job, because black blood is much more adhesive than white, and throws back with annoying persistence. When the negro gets a religion he returns directly as a hiving bee, to the first instincts of his people. Just now a wave of religion is sweeping over some of the Southern States. Up to the present, two Messiahs and one Daniel have appeared; and several human sacrifices have been offered up to these incarnations. The Daniel managed to get three young men, who he insisted were Shadrach, Meshach, and Abednego, to walk into a blast furnace; guaranteeing non-combustion. They did not return. I have seen nothing of this kind, but I have attended a negro church. The congregation were moved by the spirit to groans and tears, and one of them danced up the aisle to the mourners' bench. The motive may have been genuine. The movements of the shaken body were those of a Zanzibar stick-dance, such as you see at Aden on the coal boats; and even as I watched the people, the links that bound them to the white man snapped one by one, and I saw before me—the *hubshi* (the Woolly One) praying to the God he did not understand. Those neatly dressed folk on the benches, the gray-headed elder by the window, were savages —neither more nor less. What will the American do with the Negro? The South will not consort with him. In some States miscegenation is a penal offense. The North is every year less and less in need of his services. And he will not disappear. He will continue as a problem. His friends will urge that he is as good as the white man. His enemies . . . it is not good to be a negro in the land of the free and the home of the brave.

But this has nothing to do with San Francisco and her merry maidens, her strong, swaggering men, and her wealth of gold and pride. They bore me to a banquet in honor of a brave Lieutenant—Carlin, of the *Vandalia*—who stuck by his ship in the great cyclone at Apia and comported himself as an officer should. On that occasion—'twas at the Bohemian Club—I heard oratory with the roundest of *o*'s; and devoured a dinner the memory of which will descend with me into the hungry grave. There were about forty speeches delivered; and not one of them was average or ordinary. It was my first introduction to the American Eagle screaming for all it was worth. The Lieutenant's heroism served as a peg from which those silver-tongued ones turned themselves loose and kicked. They ransacked the clouds of sunset, the thunderbolts of Heaven, the deeps of Hell, and the splendors of the Resurrection, for tropes and metaphors, and hurled the result at the head of the guest of the evening. Never since the morning stars sang together for joy, I learned, had an amazed creation witnessed such superhuman bravery as that displayed by the American navy in the Samoa cyclone. Till earth rotted in the phosphorescent star-and-stripe slime of a decayed universe that Godlike gallantry would not be forgotten. I grieve that I cannot give the exact words. My attempt at reproducing their spirit is pale and inadequate. I sat bewildered on a coruscating Niagara of—blatherumskite. It was magnificent—it was stupendous; and I was conscious of a wicked desire to hide my face in a napkin and grin. Then, according to rule, they produced their dead, and across the snowy tablecloths dragged the corpse of every man slain in the Civil War, and hurled defiance at "our natural enemy" (England, so please you!) "with her chain of fortresses across the world." Thereafter they glorified their nation afresh, from the beginning, in case any detail should have been overlooked, and that made me uncomfortable for their sakes. How in the world can a white man, a Sahib of Our blood, stand up and plaster praise on his own country? He can think as highly as he likes, but his open-mouthed vehemence of adoration struck me almost as indelicate. My hosts talked for rather more than three hours, and at the end seemed ready for three hours more. But when the Lieutenant—such a big, brave, gentle giant!—rose to his feet, he delivered what seemed to me as the speech of the evening. I remember nearly the whole of it, and it ran something in this way: "Gentlemen—it's very good of you to give me this dinner and to tell me all these pretty things, but what I want you to understand—the fact is—what we want and what we ought to get at once is a navy—more ships—lots of 'em—" Then we howled the top of the roof off, and I, for one, fell in love with Carlin on the spot. Wallah! He was a man.

The Prince among merchants bade me take no heed to the warlike sentiments of some of the old Generals. "The sky-rockets are thrown in for effect," quoth he, "and whenever we get on our hind legs we always express a desire to chaw up England. It's a sort of family affair."

And indeed, when you come to think of it, there is no other country for the American public speaker to trample upon.

France has Germany; we have Russia; for Italy, Austria is provided; and the humblest Pathan possesses an ancestral enemy. Only America stands out of the racket; and therefore, to be in fashion, makes a sand-bag of the mother-country, and bangs her when occasion requires. "The chain of fortresses" man, a fascinating talker, explained to me after the affair that he was compelled to blow off steam. Everybody expected it. When we had chanted "The Star-Spangled Banner" not more than eight times, we adjourned. America is a very great country, but it is not yet Heaven with electric lights and plush fittings, as the speakers professed to believe. My listening mind went back to the politicians in the saloon who wasted no time in talking about free-dom, but quietly made arrangements to impose their will on the citizens. "The Judge is a great man, but give thy presents to the Clerk," as the proverb saith.

And what more remains to tell? I cannot write connectedly, because I am in love with all those girls aforesaid and some others who do not appear in the invoice. The type-writer girl is an institution of which the comic papers make much capital, but she is vastly convenient. She and a companion rent a room in a business quarter, and copy manuscript at the rate of six annas a page. Only a woman can manage a type-writing machine, because she has served apprenticeship to the sewing-machine. She can earn as much as a hundred dollars a month, and professes to regard this form of bread-winning as her natural destiny. But oh how she hates it in her heart of hearts! When I had got over the surprise of doing business and trying to give orders to a young woman of coldly clerkly aspect, intrenched behind gold-rimmed spectacles, I made inquiries concerning the pleasures of this independence. They liked it—indeed, they did. 'Twas the natural fate of almost all girls,—the recognized custom in America,—and I was a barbarian not to see it in that light.

"Well, and after?" said I. "What happens?"

"We work for our bread."

"And then what do you expect?"

"Then we shall work for our bread."

"Till you die?"

"Ye-es—unless——"

"Unless what? A man works till he dies."

"So shall we." This without enthusiasm—"I suppose."

Said the partner in the firm audaciously: "Sometimes we marry our employers—at least that's what the newspapers say." The hand banged on half a dozen of the keys of the machine at once. "Yes, I don't care. I hate it—I hate it—I *hate* it, and you needn't look so!"

The senior partner was regarding the rebel with grave-eyed reproach.

"I thought you did," said I. "I don't suppose American girls are much different from English ones in instinct."

"Isn't it Théophile Gautier who says that the only differences between country and country lie in the slang and the uniform of the police?"

Now in the name of all the Gods at once, what is one to say to a young lady (who in England would be a Person) who earns her own bread, and very naturally hates the employ, and slings out-of-the-way quotations at your head? That one falls in love with her goes without saying; but that is not enough.

A mission should be established.

V

"I walked in the lonesome even,
    And who so sad as I,
  As I saw the young men and maidens
    Merrily passing by?"

SAN FRANCISCO has only one drawback. 'Tis hard to leave. When like the pious Hans Breitmann I "cut that city by the sea" it was with regrets for the pleasant places left behind, for the men who were so clever, and the women who were so witty, for the "dives," the beer-halls, the bucket-shops, and the poker-hells where humanity was going to the Devil with shouting and laughter and song and the rattle of dice-boxes. I would fain have stayed, but I feared that an evil end would come to me when my money was all spent and I descended to the street corner. A voice inside me said: "Get out of this. Go north. Strike for Victoria and Vancouver. Bask for a day under the shadow of the old flag." So I set forth from San Francisco to Portland in Oregon, and that was a railroad run of thirty-six hours.

The Oakland railway terminus, whence all the main lines start, does not own anything approaching to a platform. A yard with a dozen or more tracks is roughly asphalted, and the traveler laden with handbags skips merrily across the metals in search of his own particular train. The bells of half a dozen shunting engines are tolling suggestively in his ears. If he is run down, so much the worse for him. "When the bell rings, look out for the locomotive." Long use has made the nation familiar and even contemptuous towards trains to an extent which God never intended. Women who in England would gather up their skirts and scud timorously over a level crossing in the country, here talk dress and babies under the very nose of the cow-catcher, and little children dally with the moving car in a manner horrible to behold. We pulled out at the wholly insignificant speed of twenty-five miles an hour through the streets of a suburb of fifty thousand, and in our progress among the carts and the children and shop fronts slew nobody; at which I was not a little disappointed.

When the negro porter bedded me up for the night and I had solved the problem of undressing while lying down,—I was much cheered by the thought that if anything happened I should have to stay where I was and wait till the kerosene lamps set the overturned car alight and burned me to death. It is easier to get out of a full theater than to leave a Pullman in haste.

By the time I had discovered that a profusion of nickle-plating, plush, and damask does not compensate for closeness and dust, the train ran into the daylight on the banks of the Sacramento River. A few windows were gingerly opened after the bunks had been reconverted into seats, but that long coffin-car was by no means ventilated, and we were a gummy, grimy crew who sat there. At six in the morning the heat was distinctly unpleasant, but seeing with the eye of the flesh that I was in Bert Harte's own country, I rejoiced. There were the pines and madrone-clad hills his miners lived and fought among; there was the heated red earth that showed whence the gold had been washed; the dry gulch, the red, dusty road where Hamblin was used to stop the stage in the intervals of his elegant leisure and superior card-play; there was the timber felled and sweating resin in the sunshine; and, above all, there was the quivering pungent heat that Bert Harte drives into your dull brain with the magic of his pen. When we stopped at a collection of packing-cases dignified by the name of a town, my felicity was complete. The name of the place was something offensive,—Amberville or Jackson-burgh,—but it owned a cast-iron fountain worthy of a town of thirty thousand. Next to the fountain was a "hotel," at least seventeen feet high including the chimney, and next to the hotel was the forest—the pine, the oak, and the untrammelled undergrowth of the hillside. A cinnamon-bear cub—Baby Sylvester in the very fur—was tied to the stump of a tree opposite the fountain; a pack-mule dozed in the dust-haze, a red-shirted miner in a slouch hat supported the hotel, a blue-shirted miner swung round the corner, and the

two went indoors for a drink. A girl came out
of the only other house but one, and shading her
eyes with a brown hand stared at the panting
train. She didn't recognize me, but I knew her
—had known her for years. She was M'liss.
She never married the schoolmaster, after all,
but stayed, always young and always fair, among
the pines. I knew Red-shirt too. He was one
of the bearded men who stood back when Ten-
nessee claimed his partner from the hands of
the Law. The Sacramento River, a few yards
away, shouted that all these things were true.
The train went on while Baby Sylvester stood
on his downy head, and M'liss swung her sun-
bonnet by the strings.

"What do you think?" said a lawyer who was
traveling with me. "It's a new world to you;
isn't it?"

"No. It's quite familiar. I was never out of
England; it's as if I saw it all."

Quick as light came the answer: " 'Yes, they
lived once thus at Venice when the miners were
the kings.' "

I loved that lawyer on the spot. We drank to
Bret Harte who, you remember, "claimed California, but California never claimed him. He's
turned English."

Lying back in state, I waited for the flying
miles to turn over the pages of the book I knew.
They brought me all I desired—from Man of no
Account sitting on a stump and playing with a

dog, to "that most sarcastic man, the quiet Mister Brown." He boarded the train from out of the woods, and there was venom and sulphur on his tongue. He had just lost a lawsuit. Only Yuba Bill failed to appear. The train had taken his employment from him. A nameless ruffian backed me into a corner and began telling me about the resources of the country, and what it would eventually become. All I remember of his lecture was that you could catch trout in the Sacramento River—the stream that we followed so faithfully.

Then rose a tough and wiry old man with grizzled hair and made inquiries about the trout. To him was added the secretary of a life-insurance company. I fancy he was traveling to rake in the dead that the train killed. But he, too, was a fisherman, and the two turned to meward. The frankness of a Westerner is delightful. They tell me that in the Eastern States I shall meet another type of man and a more reserved. The Californian always speaks of the man from the New England States as a different breed. It is our Punjab and Madras over again, but more so. The old man was on a holiday in search of fish. When he discovered a brother-loafer he proposed a confederation of rods. Quoth the insurance-agent, "I'm not staying any time in Portland, but I will introduce you to a man there who'll tell you about fishing." The two told strange tales as we slid through the forests and saw afar off the snowy head of a great mountain. There were vineyards, fruit orchards, and wheat fields where the land opened out, and every ten miles or so, twenty or thirty wooden houses and at least three churches. A large town would have a population of two thousand and an infinite belief in its own capacities. Sometimes a flaring advertisement flanked the line, calling for men to settle down, take up the ground, and make their home there. At a big town we could pick up the local newspaper, narrow as the cutting edge of a chisel and twice as keen—a journal filled with the prices of stock, notices of improved reaping and binding machines, movements of eminent citizens— "whose fame beyond their own abode extends —for miles along the Harlem road." There was not much grace about these papers, but all breathed the same need for good men, steady men who would plow, and till, and build schools for their children, and make a township in the hills. Once only I found a sharp change in the note and a very pathetic one. I think it was a young soul in trouble who was writing poetry. The editor had jammed the verses between the flamboyant advertisement of a real-estate agent—a man who sells you land and lies about it—and that of a Jew tailor who disposed of "nobby" suits at "cutthroat prices." Here are two verses; I think they tell their own story:—

"God made the pine with its root in the earth,
    Its top in the sky;
They have burned the pine to increase the worth

Of the wheat and the silver rye.
"Go weigh the cost of the soul of the pine
  Cut off from the sky;
And the price of the wheat that grows so fine
  And the worth of the silver rye!"

The thin-lipped, keen-eyed men who boarded
the train would not read that poetry, or, if they
did, would not understand. Heaven guard that
poor pine in the desert and keep "its top in the
sky!"

When the train took to itself an extra engine
and began to breathe heavily, some one said that
we were ascending the Siskiyou Mountains. We
had been climbing steadily from San Francisco,
and at last won to over four thousand feet above
sea-level, always running through forest. Then,
naturally enough, we came down, but we dropped
two thousand two hundred feet in about thirteen
miles. It was not so much the grinding of the
brakes along the train, or the sight of three curves
of track apparently miles below us, or even the
vision of a goods-train apparently just under our
wheels, or even the tunnels, that made me reflect;
it was the trestles over which we crawled,—
trestles something over a hundred feet high and
looking like a collection of match-sticks.

"I guess our timber is as much a curse as a
blessing," said the old man from Southern California. "These trestles last very well for five or
six years; then they get out of repair, and a train

goes through 'em, or else a forest fire burns 'em up."

This was said in the middle of a groaning, shivering trestle. An occasional plate-layer took a look at us as we went down, but that railway didn't waste men on inspection duty. Very often there were cattle on the track, against which the engine used a diabolical form of whistling. The old man had been a driver in his youth, and beguiled the way with cherry anecdotes of what might be expected if we fouled a young calf.

"You see, they get their legs under the cow-catcher, and that'll put an engine off the line. I remember when a hog wrecked an excursion-train and killed sixty people. 'Guess the engineer will look out, though."

There is considerably too much guessing about this large nation. As one of them put it rather forcibly: "We guess a trestle will stand forever, and we guess that we can patch up a washout on the track, and we guess the road's clear, and sometimes we guess ourselves into the depot, and sometimes we guess ourselves into Hell."

*   *   *   *   *   *

The descent brought us far into Oregon and a timber and wheat country. We drove through wheat and pine in alternate slices, but pine chiefly, till we reached Portland, which is a city of fifty thousand, possessing the electric light of course, equally, of course, devoid of pavements, and a port of entry about a hundred miles from the sea at which big steamers can load. It is a poor city that cannot say it has no equal on the Pacific coast. Portland shouts this to the pines which run down from a thousand-foot ridge clear up to the city. You may sit in a bedizened bar-room furnished with telephone and clicker, and in half an hour be in the woods.

Portland produces lumber and jig-saw fittings for houses, and beer and buggies, and bricks and biscuit; and, in case you should miss the fact, there are glorified views of the town hung up in public places with the value of the products set down in dollars. All this is excellent and exactly suitable to the opening of a new country; but when a man tells you it is civilization, you object. The first thing that the civilized man learns to do is to keep the dollars in the background, because they are only the oil of the machine that makes life go smoothly.

Portland is so busy that it can't attend to its own sewage or paving, and the four-story brick blocks front cobble-stones and plank sidewalks and other things much worse. I saw a foundation being dug out. The sewage of perhaps twenty years ago, had thoroughly soaked into the soil, and there was a familiar and Oriental look about the compost that flew up with each shovel-load. Yet the local papers, as was just and proper, swore there was no place like Portland, Oregon,

U. S. A., chronicled the performances of Oregonians, "claimed" prominent citizens elsewhere as Oregonians, and fought tooth and nail for dock, rail, and wharfage projects. And you could find men who had thrown in their lives with the city, who were bound up in it, and worked their life out for what they conceived to be its material prosperity. Pity it is to record that in this strenuous, laboring town there had been, a week before, a shooting-case. One well-known man had shot another on the street, and was now pleading self-defence, because the other man had, or the murderer thought he had, a pistol about him. Not content with shooting him dead, he squibbed off his revolver into him as he lay. I read the pleadings, and they made me ill. So far as I could judge, if the dead man's body had been found with a pistol on it, the shooter would have gone free. Apart from the mere murder, cowardly enough in itself, there was a refinement of cowardice in the plea. Here in this civilized city the surviving brute was afraid he would be shot —fancied he saw the other man make a motion to his hip-pocket, and so on. Eventually the jury disagreed. And the degrading thing was that he trial was reported by men who evidently understood all about the pistol, was tried before a jury who were versed in the etiquette of the hip-pocket, and was discussed on the streets by men equally initiate.

But let us return to more cheerful things. The

insurance-agent introduced us as friends to a real-estate man, who promptly bade us go up the Columbia River for a day while he made inquiries about fishing. There was no overwhelming formality. The old man was addressed as "California," I answered indifferently to "England" or "Johnny Bull," and the real-estate man was "Portland." This was a lofty and spacious form of address.

So California and I took a steamboat, and upon a sumptuous blue and gold morning steered up the Willamette River, on which Portland stands, into the great Columbia—the river that brings the salmon that goes into the tin that is emptied into the dish when the extra guest arrives in India. California introduced me to the boat and the scenery, showed me the "texas" the difference between a "tow-head" and a "sawyer", and the precise nature of a "slue." All I remember is a delightful feeling that Mark Twain's Huckleberry Finn and Mississippi Pilot were quite true, and that I could almost recognize the very reaches down which Huck and Jim had drifted. We were on the border line between Oregon State and Washington Territory, but that didn't matter. The Columbia was the Mississippi so far as I was concerned. We ran along the sides of wooded islands whose banks were caving in with perpetual smashes, and we skipped from one side to another of the mile-wide stream in search of a channel, exactly like a Mississippi steamer, and when we wanted to pick up or set down a passenger we

chose a soft and safe place on the shore and ran
our very snub nose against it. California spoke
to each new passenger as he came aboard and told
me the man's birthplace. A long-haired tender
of kine crushed out of the underwood, waved his
hat, and was taken aboard forthwith. "South
Carolina," said California, almost without looking
at him. "When he talks you will hear a softer
dialect than mine." And it befell as he said:
whereat I marveled, and California chuckled.
Every island in the river carried fields of rich
wheat, orchards, and a white, wooden-house; or
else, if the pines grew very thickly, a sawmill,
the tremulous whine of whose saws flickered
across the water like the drone of a tired bee.
From remarks he let fall I gathered that California
owned timber ships and dealt in lumber, had
ranches too, a partner, and everything handsome
about him; in addition to a checkered career of
some thirty-five years. But he looked almost as
disreputable a loafer as I.

"Say, young feller, we're going to see scenery
now. You shout and sing," said California, when
the bland wooded islands gave place to bolder out-
lines, and the steamer ran herself into a hornet's
nest of black-fanged rocks not a foot below the
boiling broken water. We were trying to get up
a slue, or back channel, by a short cut, and the
stern-wheel never spun twice in the same direction.
Then we hit a floating log with a jar that ran
through our system, and then, white-bellied, open-

gilled, spun by a dead salmon—a lordly twenty-pound Chinook salmon who had perished in his pride. "You'll see the salmon-wheels 'fore long," said a man who lived "way back on the Washoogle," and whose hat was spangled with trout-flies. "Those Chinook salmon never rise to fly. The canneries take them by the wheel." At the next bend we sighted a wheel—an infernal arrangement of wire-gauze compartments worked by the current and moved out from a barge in shore to scoop up the salmon as he races up the river. California swore long and fluently at the sight, and the more fluently when he was told of the weight of a good night's catch—some thousands of pounds. Think of the black and bloody murder of it! But you out yonder insist in buying tinned salmon, and the canneries cannot live by letting down lines.

About this time California was struck with madness. I found him dancing on the fore-deck shouting, "Isn't she a daisy? Isn't she a darling?" He had found a waterfall—a blown thread of white vapor that broke from the crest of a hill —a waterfall eight hundred and fifty feet high whose voice was even louder than the voice of the river. "Bridal Veil," jerked out the purser. "D—n that purser and the people who christened her! Why didn't they call her Mechlin lace Falls at fifty dollars a yard while they were at it?" said California. And I agreed with him. There are many "bridal veil" falls in this country, but few,

men say, lovelier than those that come down to
the Columbia River. Then the scenery began—
poured forth with the reckless profusion of
Nature, who when she wants to be amiable
succeeds only in being oppressively magnificent.
The river was penned between gigantic stone walls
crowned with the ruined bastions of Oriental
palaces. The stretch of green water widened and
was guarded by pine-clad hills three thousand
feet high. A wicked devil's thumb nail of rock
shot up a hundred feet in midstream. A sand-bar
of blinding white sand gave promise of flat
country that the next bend denied; for, lo! we
were running under a triple tier of fortifications,
lava-topped, pine-clothed, and terrible. Behind
them the white dome of Mount Hood ran fourteen
thousand feet into the blue, and at their feet the
river threshed among a belt of cottonwood trees.
There I sat down and looked at California half
out of the boat in his anxiety to see both sides of
the river at once. He had seen my note-book,
and it offended him. "Young feller, let her go—
and you shut your head. It's not you nor anybody
like you can put this down. Black, the novelist,
he could. He can describe salmon-fishing, *he*
can." And he glared at me as though he expected
me to go on and do likewise.

"I can't. I know it," I said humbly.

"Then thank God that you came along this
way."

We reached a little railway, on an island, which

was to convey us to a second steamer, because, as the purser explained, the river was a "trifle broken." We had a six-mile run, sitting in the sunshine on a dummy-wagon, whirled just along the edge of the river-bluffs. Sometimes we dived into the fragrant pine woods, ablaze with flowers; but we generally watched the river now narrowed into a turbulent millrace. Just where the whole body of water broke in riot over a series of cascades, the United States Government had chosen to build a lock for steamers, and the stream was one boiling, spouting mob of water. A log shot down the race, struck on a rock, split from end to end, and rolled over in white foam. I shuddered because my toes were not more than sixty feet above the log, and I feared that a stray splinter might have found me. But the train ran into the river on a sort of floating trestle, and I was upon another steamer ere I fully understood why. The cascades were not two hundred yards below us, and when we cast off to go upstream, the rush of the river, ere the wheel struck the water, dragged us as though we had been towed. Then the country opened out, and California mourned for his lost bluffs and crags, till we struck a rock wall four hundred feet high, crowned by the gigantic figure of a man watching us. On a rocky island we saw the white tomb of an old-time settler who had made his money in San Francisco, but who had chosen to be buried in an Indian burying-ground. A decayed wooden "wickyup," where the bones of the Indian dead are laid, almost touched the tomb. The river ran into a canal of basaltic rock, painted in yellow, vermilion, and green by Indanis and, by inferior brutes, adorned with advertisements of "bile beans." We had reached The Dallas—the center of a great sheep and wool district, and the head of navigation.

When an American arrives at a new town it is his bounden duty to "take it in." California swung his coat over his shoulder with the gesture of a man used to long tramps, and together, at eight in the evening, we explored The Dallas. The sun had not yet set, and it would be light for at least another hour. All the inhabitants seemed to own a little villa and one church apiece. The young men were out walking with the young maidens, the old folks were sitting on the front steps,— not the ones that led to the religiously shuttered best drawing-room, but the side-front steps,—and the husbands and wives were tying back pear trees or gathering cherries. A scent of hay reached me, and in the stillness we could hear the cattle bells as the cows came home across the lava-sprinkled fields. California swung down the wooden pavements, audibly criticising the housewives' hollyhocks and the more perfect ways of pear-grafting, and, as the young men and maidens passed, giving quaint stories of his youth. I felt that I knew all the people aforetime, I was so interested in them and their life. A woman hung over a gate talking to another woman, and as I passed I heard her say, "skirts," and again "skirts," and "I'll send you over the pattern;" and I knew they were talking dress. We stumbled upon a young couple saying good-by in the twilight, and "When shall I see you again?" quoth he; and I understood that to the doubting heart the tiny little town we paraded in twenty minutes might be as large as all London and as impassable as an armed camp. I gave them both my blessing, because "When shall I see you again?" is a question that lies very near to hearts of all the world. The last garden gate shut with a click that traveled far down the street, and the lights of the comfortable families began to shine in the confidingly uncurtained windows.

"Say, Johnny Bull, doesn't all this make you feel lonesome?" said California. "Have you got any folks at home? So've I—a wife and five children—and I'm only on a holiday."

"And I'm only on a holiday," I said, and we went back to the Spittoon-wood Hotel. Alas! for the peace and purity of the little town that I had babbled about. At the back of a shop, and discreetly curtained, was a room where the young men who had been talking to the young maidens could play poker and drink and swear, and on the shop were dime novels of bloodshed to corrupt the mind of the little boy, and prurient servant-girl-slush yarns to poison the mind of the girl. California only laughed grimly. He said that all these little one-house towns were pretty much the same all over the States.

That night I dreamed I was back in India with no place to sleep in; tramping up and down the Station mall and asking everybody, "When shall I see you again?"

VI

"The race is neither to the swift nor the battle to the strong; but time and chance cometh to all."

I HAVE lived!

The American Continent may now sink under the sea, for I have taken the best that it yields, and the best was neither dollars, love, nor real estate.

Hear now, gentlemen of the Punjab Fishing Club, who whip the reaches of the Tavi, and you who painfully import trout to Ootacamund, and I will tell you how "old man California" and I went fishing, and you shall envy.

We returned from the Dallas to Portland by the way we had come, the steamer stopping en route to pick up a night's catch of one of the salmon wheels on the river, and to deliver it at a cannery down-stream.

When the proprietor of the wheel announced that his take was two thousand two hundred and thirty pounds' weight of fish, "and not a heavy catch, neither," I thought he lied. But he sent the boxes aboard, and I counted the salmon by the hundred—huge fifty-pounders, hardly dead, scores of twenty and thirty-pounders, and a host of smaller fish.

The steamer halted at a rude wooden ware-house built on piles in a lonely reach of the river, and sent in the fish. I followed them up a scale-strewn, fishy incline that led to the cannery. The crazy building was quivering with the machinery on its floors, and a glittering bank of tin-scraps twenty feet high showed where the waste was thrown after the cans had been punched. Only Chinamen were employed on the work, and they looked like blood-besmeared yellow devils, as they crossed the rifts of sunlight that lay upon the floor. When our consignment arrived, the rough wooden boxes broke of themselves as they were dumped down under a jet of water, and the salmon burst out in a stream of quick-silver. A China-man jerked up a twenty-pounder, beheaded and detailed it with two swift strokes of a knife, flicked out its internal arrangements with a third, and cast it into a bloody-dyed tank. The headless fish leaped from under his hands as though they were facing a rapid. Other Chinamen pulled them from the vat and thrust them under a thing like a chaff-cutter, which, descending, hewed them into unseemly red gobbets fit for the can. More Chinamen with yellow, crooked fingers, jammed the stuff into the cans, which slid down some marvelous machine forthwith, soldering their own tops as they passed. Each can was hastily tested for flaws, and then sunk, with a hundred com-panions, into a vat of boiling water, there to be half cooked for a few minutes. The cans bulged slightly after the operation, and were therefore slidden along by the trolleyful to men with needles and soldering irons, who vented them, and soldered the aperture. Except for the label, the "finest Columbia salmon" was ready for the market. I was impressed, not so much with the speed of the manufacture, as the character of the factory. Inside, on a floor ninety by forty, the most civilized and murderous of machinery. Outside, three foot-steps, the thick-growing pines and the immense solitude of the hills. Our steamer only stayed twenty minutes at that place, but I counted two hundred and forty finished cans, made from the catch of the previous night, ere I left the slippery, blood-stained, scale-spangled, oily floors, and the offal-smeared Chinamen.

We reached Portland, California and I, crying for salmon, and the real-estate man, to whom we had been intrusted by "Portland" the insurance man, met us in the street saying that fifteen miles away, across country, we should come upon a place called Clackamus where we might perchance find what we desired. And California, his coat-tails flying in the wind, ran to a livery stable and chartered a wagon and team forthwith. I could push the wagon about with one hand, so light was its structure. The team was purely American—that is to say, almost human in its intelligence and docility. Some one said that the roads were not good on the way to Clackamas and warned us against smashing the springs. "Portland," who had watched the preparations, finally reckoned "he'd come along too," and under heavenly skies we three companions of a day set forth; California carefully lashing our rods into the carriage, and the bystanders overwhelming us with directions as to the sawmills we were to pass, the ferries we were to cross, and the sign-posts we were to seek signs from. Half a mile from this city of fifty thousand souls we struck (and this must be taken literally) a plank-road that would have been a disgrace to an Irish village.

Then six miles of macadamized road showed us that the team could move. A railway ran between us and the banks of the Willamette, and another above us through the mountains. All the land was dotted with small townships, and the roads were full of farmers in their town wagons, bunches of tow-haired, boggle-eyed urchins sitting in the hay behind. The men generally looked like loafers, but their women were all well dressed. Brown hussar-braiding on a tailor-made jacket does not, however, consort with hay-wagons. Then we struck into the woods along what California called a *"camina reale,"*— a good road,—and Portland a "fair track." It wound in and out among fire-blackened stumps, under pine trees, along the corners of log-fences, through hollows which must be hopeless marsh in the winter, and up absurd gradients. But nowhere throughout its length did I see any evidence of road-making. There was a track,—you

couldn't well get off it,—and it was all you could
do to stay on it. The dust lay a foot thick in
the blind ruts, and under the dust we found bits
of planking and bundles of brushwood that sent
the wagon bounding into the air. Sometimes we
crashed through bracken; anon where the blackberries grew rankest we found a lonely little ceme-
tery, the wooden rails all awry, and the pitiful
stumpy headstones nodding drunkenly at the soft
green mulleins. Then with oaths and the sound
of rent underwood a yoke of mighty bulls would
swing down a "skid" road, hauling a forty-foot
log along a rudely made slide. A valley full of
wheat and cherry trees succeeded, and halting at
a house we bought ten pound weight of luscious
black cherries for something less than a rupee
and got a drink of icy-cold water for nothing,
while the untended team browsed sagaciously by
the roadside. Once we found a wayside camp
of horse-dealers lounging by a pool, ready for a
sale or a swap, and once two sun-tanned young-
sters shot down a hill on Indian ponies, their
full creels banging from the high-pommeled
saddles. They had been fishing, and were our
brethren therefore. We shouted aloud in chorus
to scare a wild-cat; we squabbled over the reasons
that had led a snake to cross a road; we heaved
bits of bark at a venturesome chipmunk, who was
really the little gray squirrel of India and had
come to call on me; we lost our way and got the
wagon so beautifully fixed on a steep road that

we had to tie the two hind-wheels to get it down. Above all, California told tales of Nevada and Arizona, of lonely nights spent out prospecting, of the slaughter of deer and the chase of men; of woman, lovely woman, who is a firebrand in a Western city, and leads to the popping of pistols, and of the sudden changes and chances of Fortune, who delights in making the miner or the lumberman a quadruplicate millionaire, and in "busting" the railroad king. That was a day to be remembered, and it had only begun when we drew rein at a tiny farmhouse on the banks of the Clackamas and sought horse-feed and lodging ere we hastened to the river that broke over a weir not a quarter of a mile away.

Imagine a stream seventy yards broad divided by a pebbly island, running over seductive riffles, and swirling into deep, quiet pools where the good salmon goes to smoke his pipe after meals. Set such a stream amid fields of breast-high crops surrounded by hills of pine, throw in where you please quiet water, log-fenced meadows, and a hundred-foot bluff just to keep the scenery from growing too monotonous, and you will get some faint notion of the Clackamas.

Portland had no rod. He held the gaff and the whisky. California sniffed, upstream and downstream across the racing water, chose his ground, and let the gaudy spoon drop in the tail of a riffle. I was getting my rod together when I heard the joyous shriek of the reel and the yells of California, and three feet of living silver leaped into the air far across the water. The forces were engaged. The salmon tore up stream, the tense line cutting the water like a tide-rip behind him, and the light bamboo bowed to breaking. What happened after I cannot tell. California swore and prayed, and Portland shouted advice, and I did all three for what appeared to be half a day, but was in reality a little over a quarter of an hour, and sullenly our fish came home with spurts of temper, dashes head-on, and sarabands in the air; but home to the bank came he, and the remorseless reel gathered up the thread of his life inch by inch. We landed him in a little bay, and the spring-weight checked at eleven and a half pounds. Eleven and one-half pounds of fighting salmon! We danced a war-dance on the pebbles, and California caught me round the waist in a hug that went near to breaking my ribs while he shouted: "Partner! Partner! This is glory! Now you catch your fish! Twenty-four years I've waited for this!"

I went into that icy-cold river and made my cast just above a weir, and all but foul-hooked a blue and black water-snake with a coral mouth who coiled herself on a stone and hissed maledictions. The next cast—ah, the pride of it, the regal splendor of it! the thrill that ran down from finger-tip to toe! The water boiled. He broke for the fly and got it! There remained enough sense in me to give him all he wanted when he jumped not once but twenty times before the upstream flight that ran my line out to the last half-dozen turns, and I saw the nickled reel-bar glitter under the thinning green coils. My thumb was burned deep when I strove to stopper the line, but I did not feel it till later, for my soul was out in the dancing water praying for him to turn ere he took my tackle away. The prayer was heard. As I bowed back, the butt of the rod on my left hip-bone and the top joint dipping like unto a weeping willow, he turned, and I accepted each inch of slack that I could by any means get in as a favor from on High. There be several sorts of success in this world that taste well in the moment of enjoyment, but I question whether the stealthy theft of line from an able-bodied salmon who knows exactly what you are doing and why you are doing it is not sweeter than any other victory within human scope. Like California's fish, he ran at me head-on and leaped against the line, but the Lord gave me two hundred and fifty pairs of fingers in that hour. The banks and the pine trees danced dizzily round me, but I only reeled—reeled as for life—reeled for hours, and at the end of the reeling continued to give him the butt while he sulked in a pool. California was farther up the reach, and with the corner of my eye I could see him casting with long casts and much skill. Then he struck, and my fish broke for the weir at the same instant, and down the reach we came, California and I; reel answering reel, even as the morning stars sung together.

The first wild enthusiasm of capture had died away. We were both at work now in deadly earnest to prevent the lines fouling, to stall off a downstream rush for deep water just above the weir, and at the same time to get the fish into the shallow bay downstream that gave the best practicable landing. Portland bade us both be of good heart, and volunteered to take the rod from my hands. I would rather have died among the pebbles than surrender my right to play and land my first salmon, weight unknown, on an eight-ounce rod. I heard California, at my ear it seemed, gasping: "He's a fighter from Fighters-ville, sure!" as his fish made a fresh break across the stream. I saw Portland fall off a log fence, break the overhanging bank, and clatter down to the pebbles, all sand and landing-net, and I dropped on a log to rest for a moment. As I drew breath the weary hands slackened their hold, and I forgot to give him the butt. A wild scutter in the water, a plunge and a break for the headwaters of the Clackamas was my reward, and the hot toil of reeling-in with one eye under the water and the other on the top joint of the rod, was renewed. Worst of all, I was blocking California's path to the little landing-bay afore-said, and he had to halt and tire his prize where he was. "The Father of all Salmon!" he shouted. "For the love of Heaven, get your *trout* to bank, Johnny Bull." But I could no more. Even the insult failed to move me. The rest of the game was with the salmon. He suffered himself to be drawn, skipping with pretended delight at getting to the haven where I would fain have him. Yet no sooner did he feel shoal water under his ponderous belly than he backed like a torpedo-boat, and the snarl of the reel told me that my labor was in vain. A dozen times at least this happened ere the line hinted he had given up that battle and would be towed in. He was towed. The landing-net was useless for one of his size, and I would not have him gaffed. I stepped into the shallows and heaved him out with a respectful hand under the gill, for which kindness he battered me about the legs with his tail, and I felt the strength of him and was proud. California had taken my place in the shallows, his fish hard held. I was up the bank lying full length on the sweet-scented grass, and gasping in company with my first salmon caught, played and landed on an eight-ounce rod. My hands were cut and bleeding. I was dripping with sweat, spangled like harlequin with scales, wet from the waist down, nose peeled by the sun, but utterly, supremely, and consummately happy. He, the beauty, the darling, the daisy, my Salmon Bahadur, weighed twelve pounds, and I had been seven and thirty minutes bringing him to bank! He had been lightly hooked on the angle of the right jaw, and the hook had not wearied him.

That hour I sat among princes and crowned heads—greater than them all. Below the bank we heard California scuffling with his salmon, and swearing Spanish oaths. Portland and I assisted at the capture, and the fish dragged the spring-balance out by the roots. It was only constructed to weigh up to fifteen pounds. We stretched the three fish on the grass,—the eleven and a half, the twelve, and fifteen pounder,—and we swore an oath that all who came after should merely be weighed and put back again.

How shall I tell the glories of that day so that you may be interested? Again and again did California and I prance down that reach to the little bay, each with a salmon in tow, and land him in the shallows. Then Portland took my rod, and caught some ten-pounders, and my spoon was carried away by an unknown leviathan. Each fish, for the merits of the three that had died so gamely, was hastily hooked on the balance and flung back, Portland recorded the weight in a pocket-book, for he was a real-estate man. Each fish fought for all he was worth, and none more savagely than the smallest—a game little six-pounder. At the end of six hours we added up the list. Total: 16 fish, aggregate weight 142 lbs. The score in detail runs something like this—it is only interesting to those concerned: 15, 11½, 12, 10, 9¾, 8, and so forth; as I have said, nothing under six pounds, and three ten-pounders.

Very solemnly and thankfully we put up our

rods—it was glory enough for all time—and returned weeping in each other's arms—weeping tears of pure joy—to that simple bare-legged family in the packing-case house by the waterside.

The old farmer recollected days and nights of fierce warfare with the Indians—"way back in the Fifties," when every ripple of the Columbia River and her tributaries hid covert danger. God had dowered him with a queer crooked gift of expression, and a fierce anxiety for the welfare of his two little sons—tanned and reserved children who attended school daily, and spoke good English in a strange tongue.

His wife was an austere woman who had once been kindly and perhaps handsome.

Many years of toil had taken the elasticity out of step and voice. She looked for nothing better than everlasting work—the chafing detail of housework, and then a grave somewhere up the hill among the blackberries and the pines. But in her grim way she sympathized with her eldest daughter, a small and silent maiden of eighteen, who had thoughts very far from the meals she tended or the pans she scoured.

We stumbled into the household at a crisis; and there was a deal of downright humanity in that same. A bad, wicked dressmaker had promised the maiden a dress in time for a to-morrow's railway journey, and, though the barefooted Georgie, who stood in very wholesome awe of his sister, had scoured the woods on a pony in search, that dress never arrived. So with sorrow in her heart, and a hundred Sister Anne glances up the road, she waited upon the strangers, and, I doubt not, cursed them for the wants that stood between her and her need for tears. It was a genuine little tragedy. The mother in a heavy, passionless voice rebuked her impatience, yet sat bowed over a heap of sewing for the daughter's benefit.

These things I beheld in the long marigold-scented twilight and whispering night, loafing round the little house with California, who unfolded himself like a lotus to the moon; or in the little boarded bunk that was our bedroom, swapping tales with Portland and the old man. Most of the yarns began in this way:

"Red Larry was a bull-puncher back of Lone County, Montana," or "There was a man riding the trail met a jack-rabbit sitting in a cactus," or "'Bout the time of the San Diego land boom, a woman from Monterey." etc.

You can try to piece out for yourselves what sort of stories they were.

And next day California took me under his wing and told me we were going to see a city smitten by a boom, and catch trout. So we took a train and killed a cow—she wouldn't get out of the way, and the locomotive "chanced" her and slew—and crossing into Washington Territory won the town of Tacoma, which stands at the head of Puget Sound upon the road to Alaska and Vancouver.

California was right. Tacoma was literally staggering under a boom of the boomiest. I do not quite remember what her natural resources were supposed to be, though every second man shrieked a selection in my ear. They included coal and iron, carrots, potatoes, lumber, shipping, and a crop of thin newspapers all telling Portland that her days were numbered. California and I struck the place at twilight. The rude boarded pavements of the main streets rumbled under the heels of hundreds of furious men all actively engaged in hunting drinks and eligible corner-lots. They sought the drinks first. The street itself alternated five-story business blocks of the later and more abominable forms of architecture with board shanties. Overhead the drunken telegraph, telephone, and electric light wires tangled on the tottering posts whose butts were half-whittled through by the knife of the loafer. Down the muddy, grimy, unmetaled thoroughfare ran a horse-car line—the metals three inches above road level. Beyond this street rose many hills, and the town was thrown like a broken set of dominoes over all. A steam tramway—it left the track the only time I used it —was nosing about the hills, but the most prominent features of the landscape where the foundations in brick and stone of a gigantic opera house and the blackened stumps of the pines. California sized up the town with one comprehensive glance. "Big boom," said he; and a few instants later: "About time to step off, I think," meaning thereby that the boom had risen to its limit, and it would be expedient not to meddle with it. We passed down ungraded streets that ended abruptly in a fifteen-foot drop and a nest of brambles; along pavements that beginning in pine-plank ended in the living tree; by hotels with Turkish mosque trinketry on their shameless tops, and the pine stumps at their very doors; by a female seminary, tall, gaunt and red, which a native of the town bade us marvel at, and we marveled; by houses built in imitation of the ones on Nob Hill, San Francisco,—after the Dutch fashion; by other houses, plenteously befouled with jig-saw work, and others flaring with the castle-mented, battlemented bosh of the wooden Gothic school.

"You can tell just about when those fellers had their houses built," quoth California. "That one yonder wanted to be *I*talian, and his architect built him what he wanted. The new houses with the low straddle roofs and windows pitched in sideways and red brick walls are Dutch. That's the latest idea. I can read the history of the town." I had no occasion so to read. The natives were only too glad and too proud to tell me. The hotel walls bore a flaming panorama of Tacoma in which by the eye of faith I saw a faint resemblance to the real town. The hotel sta-

tionery advertised that Tacoma bore on its face
all the advantages of the highest civilization, and
the newspapers sang the same tune in a louder
key. The real-estate agents were selling house-
lots on unmade streets miles away for thousands
of dollars. On the streets—the rude, crude
streets, where the unshaded electric light was
fighting with the gentle northern twilight—men
were babbling of money, town lots, and again
money—how Alf or Ed had done such and such
a thing that had brought him so much money;
and round the corner in a creaking boarded hall
the red-jerseyed Salvationists were calling upon
mankind to renounce all and follow their noisy
God. The men dropped in by twos and threes,
listened silently for a while, and as silently went
their way, the cymbals clashing after them in vain.
I think it was the raw, new smell of fresh saw-
dust everywhere pervading the air that threw
upon me a desolating homesickness. It brought
back in a moment all remembrances of that terrible first night at school when the establishment
has been newly whitewashed, and a soft smell of
escaping gas mingles with the odor of trunks and
wet overcoats. I was a little boy, and the school
was very new. A vagabond among collarless
vagabonds, I loafed up the street, looking into
the fronts of little shops where they sold slop
shirts at fancy prices, which shops I saw later
described in the papers as "great." California
had gone off to investigate on his own account,

and presently returned, laughing noiselessly. "They are all mad here," he said, "all mad. A man nearly pulled a gun on me because I didn't agree with him that Tacoma was going to whip San Francisco on the strength of carrots and potatoes. I asked him to tell me what the town produced, and I couldn't get anything out of him except those two darned vegetables. Say, what do you think?"

I responded firmly, "I'm going into British territory a little while—to draw breath."

"I'm going up the Sound, too, for a while," said he, "but I'm coming back—coming back to our salmon on the Clackamas. A man has been pressing me to buy real estate here. Young feller, don't you buy real estate here."

California disappeared with a kindly wave of his overcoat into worlds other than mine,—good luck go with him, for he was a true sportsman! —and I took a steamer up Puget Sound for Vancouver, which is the terminus of the Canadian Pacific Railway. That was a queer voyage. The water, landlocked among a thousand islands, lay still as oil under our bows, and the wake of the screw broke up the unquivering reflections of pines and cliffs a mile away. 'Twas as though we were trampling on glass. No one, not even the Government, knows the number of islands in the Sound. Even now you can get one almost for the asking; can build a house, raise sheep, catch Salmon, and become a king on a small scale—

your subjects the Indians of the reservation, who glide among the islets in their canoes and scratch their hides monkey-wise by the beach. A Sound Indian is unlovely, and only by accident picturesque. His wife drives the canoe, but he himself is so thorough a mariner that he can spring up in his cockle-craft and whack his wife over the head with a paddle without tipping the whole affair into the water. This I have seen him do unprovoked. I fancy it must have been to show off before the whites.

Have I told you anything about Seattle—the town that was burned out a few weeks ago when the insurance men at San Francisco took their losses with a grin? In the ghostly twilight, just as the forest fires were beginning to glare from the unthrifty islands, we struck it—struck it heavily, for the wharves had all been burned down, and we tied up where we could, crashing into the rotten foundations of a boat house as a pig roots in high grass. The town, like Tacoma, was built upon a hill. In the heart of the business quarters there was a horrible black smudge, as though a Hand had come down and rubbed the place smooth. I know now what being wiped out means. The smudge seemed to be about a mile long, and its blackness was relieved by tents in which men were doing business with the wreck of the stock they had saved. There were shouts and counter-shouts from the steamer to the temporary wharf, which was laden with shingles for roofing, chairs, trunks, provision-boxes, and all the lath and string arrangements out of which a western town is made. This is the way the shouts ran:—

"Oh, George! What's the best with you?"

"Nawthin'. Got the old safe out. She's burned to a crisp. Books all gone."

"Save anythin'?"

"Bar'l o' crackers and my wife's bonnet. Goin' to start store on them though."

"Bully for you. Where's that Emporium? I'll drop in."

"Corner what used to be Fourth and Main— little brown tent close to militia picket. Sa-ay! We're under martial law, an' all the saloons are shut down."

"Best for you, George. Some men gets crazy with a fire, an' liquor makes 'em crazier."

"'Spect any creator-condemned son of a female dog who has lost all his fixin's in a conflagration is going to put ice on his head an' run for Congress, do you? How'd you like us act?"

The Job's comforter on the steamer retired into himself.

"Oh, George" dived into the bar for a drink.

P. S.—Among many curiosities I have unearthed one. It was a Face on a steamer—a face above a pointed straw-colored beard, a face with thin lips and eloquent eyes. We conversed, and presently I got at the ideas of the Face. It was, though it lived for nine months of the year in the wilds of Alaska and British Columbia, an authority on the canon law of the Church of England—a zealous and bitter upholder of the supremacy of the aforesaid Church. Into my amazed ears, as the steamer plodded through the reflections of the stars, it poured the battle-cry of the Church Militant here on earth, and put forward as a foul injustice that in the prisons of British Columbia the Protestant chaplain did not always belong to the Church. The Face had no official connection with the august body, and by force of his life very seldom attended service.

"But," said he, proudly, "I should think it direct disobedience to the orders of my Church if I attended any other places of worship than those prescribed. I was once for three months in a place where there was only a Wesleyan Methodist chapel, and I never set foot in it once, Sir. Never once. 'Twould have been heresy. Rank heresy."

And as I leaned over the rail methought that all the little stars in the water were shaking with austere merriment! But it may have been only the ripple of the steamer, after all.

VII

"But who shall chronicle the ways
   Of common folk, the nights and days
   Spent with rough goatherds on the snows,
   And travelers come whence no man knows?"

THIS day I know how a deserter feels. Here
in Victoria, a hundred and forty miles out of
America, the mail brings me news from our
Home—the land of regrets. I was enjoying myself by the side of a trout-stream, and I feel in-
clined to apologize for every rejoicing breath I
drew in the diamond clear air. The sickness,
they said, is heavy with you; from Rewari to
the south good men are dying. Two names come
in by the mail of two strong men dead—men
that I dined and jested with only a little time ago,
and it seems unfair that I should be here, cut off
from the chain-gang and the shot-drill of our
weary life. After all, there is no life like it that
we lead over yonder. Americans are Americans,
and there are millions of them; English are English; but we of India are Us all the world over,
knowing the mysteries of each other's lives and
sorrowing for the death of a brother. How can
I sit down and write to you of the mere joy of
being alive? The news has killed the pleasure
of the day for me, and I am ashamed of my-

self. There are seventy brook trout lying in
a creel, fresh drawn from Harrison Hot Springs,
and they do not console me. They are like the
stolen apples that clinch the fact of a bad boy's
playing truant. I would sell them all, with my
heritage in the woods and air and the delight
of meeting new and strange people, just to be
back again in the old galling harness, the heat
and the dust, the gatherings in the evenings by
the flooded tennis-courts, the ghastly dull dinners
at the Club when the very last woman has been
packed off to the hills and the four or five surviving men ask the doctor the symptoms of incu-
bating smallpox. I should be troubled in body,
but at peace in the soul. O excellent and toil-
worn public of mine—men of the brotherhood,
griffins new joined from the February troopers,
and gentlemen waiting for your off reckonings—
take care of yourselves and keep well! It hurts
so when any die. There are so few of Us, and
we know one another too intimately.

*   *   *   *   *   *

Vancouver three years ago was swept off by
fire in sixteen minutes, and only one house was
left standing. To-day it has a population of
fourteen thousand people, and builds its houses
out of brick with dressed granite fronts. But
a great sleepiness lies on Vancouver as compared
with an American town; men don't fly up and
down the streets telling lies, and the spittoons in

the delightfully comfortable hotel are unused; the baths are free and their doors are unlocked. You do not have to dig up the hotel clerk when you want to bathe, which shows the inferiority of Vancouver. An American bade me notice the absence of bustle, and was alarmed when in a loud and audible voice I thanked God for it. "Give me granite—hewn granite and peace," quoth I, "and keep your deal boards and bustle for yourselves."

The Canadian Pacific terminus is not a very gorgeous place as yet, but you can be shot directly from the window of the train into the liner that will take you in fourteen days from Vancouver to Yokohama. The *Parthia,* of some five thousand tons, was at her berth when I came, and the sight of the ex-Cunard on what seemed to be a little lake was curious. Except for certain currents which are not much mentioned, but which make the entrance rather unpleasant for sailing-boats, Vancouver possesses an almost perfect harbor. The town is built all round and about the harbor, and young as it is, its streets are better than those of western America. Moreover, the old flag waves over some of the buildings, and this is cheering to the soul. The place is full of Englishmen who speak the English tongue correctly and with clearness, avoiding more blasphemy than is necessary, and taking a respectable length of time to getting outside their drinks. These advantages and others that I have heard about, such as the construction of elaborate workshops and the like by the Canadian Pacific in the near future, moved me to invest in real estate. He that sold it me was a delightful English Boy who, having tried for the Army and failed, had somehow meandered into a real-estate office, where he was doing well. I couldn't have bought it from an American. He would have overstated the case and proved me the possessor of the original Eden. All the Boy said was: "I give you my word it isn't on a cliff or under water, and before long the town ought to move out that way. I'd advise you to take it." And I took it as easily as a man buys a piece of tobacco. *Me voici,* owner of some four hundred well developed pines, a few thousand tons of granite scattered in blocks at the roots of the pines, and a sprinkling of earth. That's a town-lot in Vancouver. You or your agent hold to it till property rises, then sell out and buy more land further out of town and repeat the process. I do not quite see how this sort of thing helps the growth of a town, but the English Boy says that it is the "essence of speculation," so it must be all right. But I wish there were fewer pines and rather less granite on my ground. Moved by curiosity and the lust of trout, I went seventy miles up the Canadian Pacific in one of the cross-Continent cars, which are cleaner and less stuffy than the Pullman. A man who goes all the way across Canada is liable to be disappointed—not in the scenery, but in the progress of the country. So a batch of wandering politicians from England told me. They even went so far as to say that Eastern Canada was a failure and unprofitable. The place didn't move, they complained, and whole counties—they said provinces—lay under the rule of the Roman Catholic priests, who took care that the people should not be over-cumbered with the good things of this world to the detriment of their souls. My interest was in the line—the real and accomplished railway which is to throw actual fighting troops into the East some day when our hold of the Suez Canal is temporarily loosened.

All that Vancouver wants is a fat earthwork fort upon a hill,—there are plenty of hills to choose from,—a selection of big guns, a couple of regiments of infantry, and later on a big arsenal. The raw self-consciousness of America would be sure to make her think these arrangements intended for her benefit, but she could be enlightened. It is not seemly to leave unprotected the head-end of a big railway; for through Victoria and Esquimalt, our naval stations on Vancouver Island, are very near, so also is a place called Vladivostok, and though Vancouver Narrows are strait, they allow room enough for a man-of-war. The people—I did not speak to more than two hundred of them—do not know about Russia or military arrangements. They are trying to open trade with Japan in lumber, and are raising fruit, wheat, and sometimes minerals.

All of them agree that we do not yet know the
resources of British Columbia, and all joyfully
bade me note the climate, which was distinctly
warm. "We never have killing cold here. It's
the most perfect climate in the world." Then
there are three perfect climates, for I have tasted
'em—California, Washington Territory, and
British Columbia. I cannot say which is the
loveliest.

When I left by steamer and struck across the
Sound to our naval station at Victoria, Vancouver
Island, I found in that quite English town of
beautiful streets quite a colony of old men doing
nothing but talking, fishing, and loafing at the
Club. That means that the retired go to Victoria.
On a thousand a year pension a man would be a
millionaire in these parts, and for four hundred
he could live well. It was at Victoria they told
me the tale of the fire in Vancouver. How the
inhabitants of New Westminster, twelve miles
from Vancouver, saw a glare in the sky at six
in the evening, but thought it was a forest fire;
how later bits of burnt paper flew about their
streets, and they guessed that evil had happened;
how an hour later a man rode into the city crying that there was no Vancouver left. All had
been wiped out by the flames in sixteen minutes.
How, two hours later, the Mayor of New Westminster having voted nine thousand dollars from
the Municipal funds, relief-wagons with food and
blankets were pouring into where Vancouver

stood. How fourteen people were supposed to have died in the fire, but how even now when they laid new foundations the workmen unearthed charred skeletons, many more than fourteen. "That night," said the teller, "all Vancouver was houseless. The wooden town had gone in a breath. Next day they began to build in brick, and you have seen what they have achieved."

The sight afar off of three British men-of-war and a torpedo-boat consoled me as I returned from Victoria to Tacoma and discovered *en route* that I was surfeited with scenery. There is a great deal in the remark of a discontented traveler: "When you have seen a fine forest, a bluff, a river, and a lake you have seen all the scenery of western America. Sometimes the pine is three hundred feet high, and sometimes the rock is, and sometimes the lake is a hundred miles long. But it's all the same, don't you know. I'm getting sick of it." I dare not say getting sick. I'm only tired. If Providence could distribute all this beauty in little bits where people most wanted it—among you in India,—it would be well. But it is en masse, overwhelming, with nobody but the tobacco-chewing captain of a river steamboat to look at it. Men said if I went to Alaska I should see islands even more wooded, snow-peaks loftier, and rivers more lovely than those around me. That decided me not to go to Alaska. I went east—east to Montana, after another horrible night in Tacoma among the men who spat. Why does the Westerner spit? It can't amuse him, and it doesn't interest his neighbor.

But I am beginning to mistrust. Everything good as well as everything bad is supposed to come from the East. Is there a shooting-scrape between prominent citizens? Oh, you'll find nothing of that kind in the East. Is there a more than usually revolting lynching? They don't do that in the East. I shall find out when I get there whether this unnatural perfection be real.

Eastward then to Montana I took my way for the Yellowstone National Park, called in the guide-books "Wonderland." But the real Wonderland began in the train. We were a merry crew. One gentleman announced his intention of paying no fare and grappled the conductor, who neatly cross-buttocked him through a double plate-glass window. His head was cut open in four or five places. A doctor on the train hastily stitched up the biggest gash, and he was dropped at a wayside station, spurting blood at every hair—a scarlet-headed and ghastly sight. The conductor guessed that he would die, and volunteered the information that there was no profit in monkeying with the North Pacific Railway.

Night was falling when we cleared the forests and sailed out upon a wilderness of sage brush. The desolations of Montgomery, the wilderness of Sind, the hummock-studded desert of Bikaneer, are joyous and homelike compared to the

impoverished misery of the sage. It is blue, it
is stunted, it is dusty. It wraps the rolling hills
as a mildewed shroud wraps the body of a long-
dead man. It makes you weep for sheer loneliness, and there is no getting away from it. When
Childe Roland came to the dark Tower he trav-
ersed the sage brush.

Yet there is one thing worse than sage un-
adulterated and that is a prairie city. We stopped
at Pasco Junction, and a man told me that it was
the Queen City of the Prairie. I wish Americans
didn't tell such useless lies. I counted fourteen
or fifteen frame-houses, and a portion of a road
that showed like a bruise on the untouched sur-
face of the blue sage, running away and away up
to the setting sun. The sailor sleeps with a half-
inch plank between himself and death. He is at
home beside the handful of people who curl themselves up o' nights with nothing but a frail scant-
ling, almost as thin as a blanket, to shut out the
unmeasurable loneliness of the sage.

When the train stopped on the road, as it did
once or twice, the solid silence of the sage got
up and shouted at us. It was like a nightmare,
and one not in the least improved by having to
sleep in an emigrant-car; the regularly ordained
sleepers being full. There was a row in our car
toward morning, a man having managed to get
querulously drunk in the night. Up rose a Cor-
nishman with a red head full of strategy, and
strapped the obstreperous one, smiling largely as

he did so, and a delicate little woman in a far bunk watched the fray and called the drunken man a "damned hog," which he certainly was, though she needn't have put it quite so coarsely. Emigrant cars are clean, but the accommodation is as hard as a plank bed.

Later we laid our bones down to crossing the Rockies. An American train can climb up the side of a house if need be, but it is not pleasant to sit in it. We clomb till we struck violent cold and an Indian Reservation, and the noble savage came to look at us. He was a Flathead and unlovely. Most Americans are charmingly frank about the Indian. "Let us get rid of him as soon as possible," they say. "We have no use for him." Some of the men I meet have a notion that we in India are exterminating the native in the same fashion, and I have been asked to fix a date for the final extinguishment of the Aryan. I answer that it will be a long business. Very many Americans have an offensive habit of referring to natives as "heathen." Mahometans and Hindus are heathen alike in their eyes, and they vary the epithet with "pagan" and "idolater." But this is beside the matter, which is the Stampede Tunnel—our actual point of crossing the Rockies. Thank Heaven, I need never take that tunnel again! It is about two miles long, and in effect is nothing more than the gallery of a mine shored with timber and lighted with electric lamps. Black darkness would be preferable, for

youngster conceives to be wit has offended a
sensibility; and another deftly slides the decanters
beyond him as they circle round the table. You
know the feeling of discomfort—pity mingled
with aversion—over the boy who is making an
exhibition of himself. The same emotion came
back to me, when an old man who ought to have
known better appealed from time to time for ad-
miration of his pitiful sentiments. It was right
in his mind to insult, to maim, and to kill; right
to evade the law where it was strong and to
trample over it where it was weak; right to
swindle in politics, to lie in affairs of State, and
commit perjury in matters of municipal admin-
istration. The car was full of little children,
utterly regardless of their parents, fretful,
peevish, spoilt beyond anything I have ever seen in
Anglo-India. They in time would grow up into
men such as sat in the smoker, and had no regard
for the law, men who would conduct papers sid-
ing "with defiance of any and every law." But
it's of no consequence, as Mr. Toots says.

During the descent of the Rockies we jour-
neyed for a season on a trestle only two hundred
and eighty-six feet high. It was made of iron,
but up till two years ago a wooden structure bore
up the train, and was used long after it had been
condemned by the civil engineers. Some day the
iron one will come down, just as Stampede Tunnel will, and the results will be even more start-
ling.

Late in the night we ran over a skunk—ran over it in the dark. Everything that has been said about the skunk is true. It is an Awesome Stink.